RON FRY'S **HOW TO STUDY** PROGRAM

"ACE" ANY TEST

FOURTH EDITION

BY **RON FRY**

CAREER PRESS
Franklin Lakes, NJ

"ACE" ANY TEST, 4TH EDITION
Cover design by Design Solutions
Printed in the U.S.A. by Book-mart Press

To order this title, please call toll-free 1-800-CAREER-1 (NJ and Canada: 201-848-0310) to order using VISA or MasterCard, or for further information on books from Career Press.

The Career Press, Inc., 3 Tice Road, PO Box 687,
Franklin Lakes, NJ 07417
www.careerpress.com

Library of Congress Cataloging-in-Publication Data

Fry, Ronald W.
"Ace" any test / by Ron Fry.—4th ed.
p. cm.
Includes index.
ISBN 1-56414-460-7 (paper)
1. Examinations—United States—Study guides. 2. Test-taking skills—United States. I. Title.

LB3060.57 F79 2000
371.26—dc21 00-031213

Contents

"ACE" ANY TEST

"ACE" ANY TEST

FOREWORD

There *Will* Be a Quiz on This

THIS YEAR MARKS another major milestone in the decade-long evolution of my ***How to Study Program***—the reissuance of new editions of the key volumes: ***How to Study*** itself, now in a fifth edition; fourth editions of ***Improve Your Memory, Improve Your Reading, Improve Your Writing,*** and ***"Ace" Any Test;*** and a second edition of ***Get Organized.*** (***Take Notes, Manage Your Time,*** and ***Use Your Computer,*** though still available, were not revised this year.)

I am truly proud, though somewhat amazed, that ***How to Study*** itself is now well into its second decade. While all authors want to believe their books will last forever, most wind up in the remainder bin far sooner than we would ever like (or admit).

I cannot take very much credit for these books' longevity. Unfortunately, the state of affairs that existed in 1988 has not improved—teachers are still underpaid, students are still undertaught, schools are still underfunded, and study skills are still underutilized. As a result, my ***How to Study Program*** is, for many of you, parents and students alike, the only source of information about the vital skills needed to succeed both in school and in life.

So who are you?

A number of you are students, not just the high school students I always thought were my readers, but also college students (a rousing plug for their high school preparation) and *junior* high school students (which says something far more positive about their motivation and eventual success).

Many of you reading this are adults. Some of you are returning to school, and some of you are long out of school, but if you could learn *now* the study skills your teachers never taught you, you would do better in your careers—especially if you knew how to manage that group project or complete that report *before* the deadline.

All too many of you are parents with the same lament: "How do I get Jill to do better in school? She didn't even get the minimum score (400) on the SAT."

I want to briefly take the time to address every one of the audiences for this book and discuss some of the factors particular to each of you.

If you're a high school student

You should be particularly comfortable with both the language and format of this book—its relatively short sentences and paragraphs, occasionally humorous (hopefully) headings and subheadings, and a reasonable but certainly not outrageous vocabulary. I wrote it with you in mind!

If you're a junior high school student

You are trying to learn how to study at *precisely* the right time. Sixth, 7th, and 8th grades—before that sometimes-cosmic leap to high school—are without a doubt the period in which all these study skills should be mastered. If you're serious enough about studying to be reading this book, I doubt you'll have trouble with the concepts or the language.

If you're a "traditional" college student...

...who pretty much went right on to college from high school, how'd you manage *that* leap without mastering test-taking techniques?

Well, here you are, facing more and tougher tests than ever before. Don't worry—***"Ace" Any Test*** will help you, no matter how tough your professors think they are.

If you're the parent of a student of any age

Your child's school is probably doing little if anything to teach him or her how to study. Which means he or she is not learning how to *learn*. And that means he or she is not learning how to *succeed*.

Should the schools be accomplishing that? Absolutely. After all, we spend $275 billion on elementary and secondary education in this country, *an average of $6,000 per student per year*. We ought to be getting more for that money than possible graduation, some football cheers, and an autographed yearbook.

What can parents do?

There are probably even more dedicated parents out there than dedicated students, because the first phone call at any of my radio or TV appearances usually comes from a sincere and worried parent asking, "What can I do to help my kid do better in school?" Okay, here they are, the rules for parents of students of any age:

1. **Set up a homework area.** Free of distraction, well-lit, all necessary supplies handy.
2. **Set up a homework routine.** When and where it gets done. Same time, same place, every day.
3. **Set homework priorities.** Actually, just make the point that homework *is* the priority—before a date, before TV, before going out to play, before whatever.
4. **Make reading a habit**—for them, certainly, but also for yourselves, presuming it isn't already. Kids will inevitably do what you *do*, not what you *say* (even if you say *not* to do what you *do*). So if you keep nagging them to read while *you* turn on the eighth sitcom of the night, what message do you think you're giving them?
5. **Turn off the TV.** Or, at the very least, severely limit when and how much TV-watching is appropriate. This may be the toughest one. Believe me, I'm the father of an 11-year-old. I know. Do your best.
6. **Talk to the teachers.** Find out what your kids are supposed to be learning. If you don't, you can't really supervise. You might even be teaching them things at odds with what the teacher's trying to do.
7. **Encourage and motivate,** but don't nag them to do their homework. It doesn't work.

8. **Supervise their work,** but don't fall into the trap of *doing* their homework for them.
9. **Praise them to succeed,** but don't overpraise them for mediocre work. Kids know when you're slinging it.
10. **Convince them of reality.** (This is for older students.) Okay, I'll admit it's almost as much of a stretch as turning off the TV, but learning and believing that the real world will not care about their grades but measure them solely by what they know and what they can do is a lesson that will save many tears (probably yours). It's probably never too early to (carefully) let your boy or girl genius get the message that life is not fair.
11. **If you can afford it, get your kid(s) a computer** and all the software they can handle. There really is no avoiding it: Your kids, whatever their age, must master technology (computers) in order to survive, let alone succeed, in and after school. There's even new empirical data to back up all the braying: A recent decade-long study has shown that kids who master computers learn faster and earn higher test scores.
12. **Turn off the TV already!**
13. **Get wired.** The Internet is the greatest invention of our age and an unbelievable tool for students of any age. While it's impossible to list even a smattering of helpful sites in a book this brief, parents of elementary and high school students should check out the following:

    www.schoolwork.org
    www.sunsite.berkeley.edu/KidsClick
    www.HomeworkCentral.com
      (a division of *www.bigchalk.com*)
    www.iln.net
    www.tutor.com

The importance of your involvement

Don't for a minute underestimate the importance of *your* commitment to your child's success: Your involvement in your child's education is absolutely essential to his or her eventual success. Surprisingly enough, the results of every study done in the last three decades about what affects a child's success in school clearly demonstrate that only one factor *overwhelmingly* affects it, every time: parental involvement. Not the size of the school, the number of language labs, how many of the students go on to college, how many great teachers there are (or lousy ones). All factors, yes. *But none as significant as the effect you can have.*

You can help tremendously, *even if you were not a great student, even if you never learned great study skills.* Learn with your child—not only will it help him or her in school, it will help *you* on the job, whatever your field.

If you're a nontraditional student

If you're going back to high school, college, or graduate school at age 25, 45, 65, or 85—you probably need the help my books offer more than anyone! Why? Because the longer you've been out of school, the more likely you don't remember what you've forgotten. And you've probably forgotten what you're supposed to remember! As much as I emphasize that it's rarely too early to learn good study habits, I must also emphasize that it's never too *late.*

Some random thoughts about learning

Learning shouldn't be painful and certainly doesn't have to be boring, though it's far too often both. However, it's not necessarily going to be wonderful and painless, either. Sometimes you actually have to work hard to figure something out or get a project done. That *is* reality.

It's also reality that everything isn't readily apparent or easily understandable. Confusion reigns. Tell yourself that's okay and learn how to get past it. Heck, if you actually think you should understand everything you read the first time through, you're kidding yourself. Learning something slowly doesn't mean there's something wrong with you. It may be a subject that virtually everybody learns slowly. A good student doesn't panic when something doesn't seem to be getting through the haze. He just takes his time, follows whatever steps apply, and remains confident that the light bulb will indeed inevitably go on.

How many times have you said to yourself, "I don't know why I'm bothering trying to learn this calculus (or algebra, geometry, physics, chemistry, history, whatever). I'll *never* use this again!"? I hate to burst bubbles, but unless you've got a patent on some great new fortune-telling device, you have *no clue* what you're going to need to know tomorrow or next week, let alone next year or in a decade.

I've been amazed in my own life how things I did with no specific purpose in mind (except probably to earn money) turned out years later to be not just invaluable to my life or career but essential. (Okay, I'll admit it: I haven't used a differential equation in 20 years, but, hey, you never know!)

So learn it *all*. And don't be surprised if the subject you'd vote "least likely to ever be useful" winds up being the key to *your* fame and fortune.

There *are* other study guides

Though I immodestly maintain my ***How to Study Program*** to be the most helpful to the most people, there are certainly lots of other purported study books out there. Unfortunately, I don't think many of them deliver what they promise. In fact, I'm actually getting mad at the growing number of study guides out there claiming to be "the sure way to straight A's" or something of the sort. These are also the books that dismiss reasonable alternative ways to study and learn with, "Well, that never worked for me," as if that is a valid reason to dismiss it, as if we should *care* that it didn't work for the author.

Inevitably, these other books promote the authors' "system," which usually means what *they* did to get through school. This "system," whether basic and traditional or wildly quirky, may or may not work for you. So what do you do if "their" way of taking notes makes no sense to you? Or you master their highfalutin "Super Student Study Symbols" and still get C's?

Needless to say, don't read *my* books looking for the Truth—that single, inestimable system of "rules" that works for everyone. You won't find it, 'cause there's no such bird. You *will* find a plethora of techniques, tips, tricks, gimmicks, and what-have-you, some or all of which may work for you, some of which won't. Pick and choose, change and adapt, figure out what works for you. Because *you* are the one responsible for creating *your* study system, *not me*.

Yes, I'll occasionally point out "my way" of doing something. I may even suggest that I think it offers some clear advantages to all the alternative ways of accomplishing the same thing. But that *doesn't* mean it's some carved-in-stone, deviate-from-the-sacred-Ron-Fry-study-path-under-penalty-of-a-writhing-death kind of rule.

I've used the phrase "study smarter, not harder" as a sort of catch phrase in promotion and publicity for the ***How to Study Program*** for nearly a decade. So what does it mean to you? Does it mean I guarantee you'll spend less time studying? Or that the least amount of time is best? Or that studying isn't ever supposed to be difficult?

Hardly. It does mean that studying inefficiently is wasting time that could be spent doing other (okay, probably more *fun)* things and that getting your studying done as quickly and efficiently as possible is a realistic, worthy, and *attainable* goal. I'm no stranger to hard work, but I'm not a monastic dropout who thrives on self-flagellation. I try not to work harder than I have to!

www.study.com

In 1988, when I wrote the first edition of ***How to Study,*** I composed it, formatted it, and printed it on (gasp) a personal computer. Yes, boys and girls, in those halycon days, I was surfing a wave that didn't hit shore for a few more years. Most people did *not* have a computer, let alone a neighborhood network and DSL, or surf the Web (whatever that was), or chat online, or Instant Message their friends, or...you get the point.

In case you've been living in a cave that Bill Gates forgot to wire, those days are very dead and gone. And you should cheer, even if you aren't sure what DOS was (is? could be?). Because the spread of the personal computer and, even more, the Internet, has taken studying from the Dark Ages to the Info Age in merely a decade.

As a result, you will find all of my books assume you have a computer and know how to use it—for note-taking, reading, paper-writing, researching, and much more. There are many tasks that may be harder on a computer—and I'll point them out—but don't believe for a second that a computer won't help you tremendously, whatever your age, whatever your grades.

As for the Internet, it has absolutely revolutionized research. Whether you're writing a paper, putting together a reading list, studying for the SAT, or just trying to organize your life, it has become a more valuable tool than the greatest library in the world. Heck, it *is* the greatest library in the world...and more. So if you aren't Internet savvy (yes, I'm talking to the parents out there, couldn't you tell?), admit you're a dummy, get a book (over the Internet, of course), and get wired. You'll be missing far too much—and be studying far harder—without it.

In case you were wondering

Before we get on with all the tips and techniques necessary to make tests quake when they see you coming, let me make two important points about all of my study books.

First, I believe in gender equality, in writing as well as in life. Unfortunately, I find constructions such as "he and she," "s/he," "womyn," and other such stretches to be sometimes painfully awkward. I have therefore attempted to sprinkle pronouns of both genders throughout the text.

Second, you will find many of my pieces of advice, examples, lists, phrases, and sections spread throughout two or more of the books. Certainly ***How to Study,*** which is an overview of all the study skills, necessarily contains, though in summarized form, some of each of the other eight books.

The repetition is unavoidable. While I urge everyone to read all the books in the series, but especially ***How to Study,*** they *are* nine individual books. And many people only buy one of them. Consequently, I must include in each the pertinent material *for that topic,* even if that material is then repeated in a second or even a third book.

That said, I can guarantee that the nearly 1,200 pages of my ***How to Study Program*** contain the most wide-ranging, comprehensive, and complete system of studying ever published. I have attempted to create a system that is usable, that is useful, that is practical, that is learnable. One that *you* can use—whatever your age, whatever your level of achievement, whatever your IQ—to start doing better in school, in work, and in life *immediately*.

—Ron Fry
May 2000

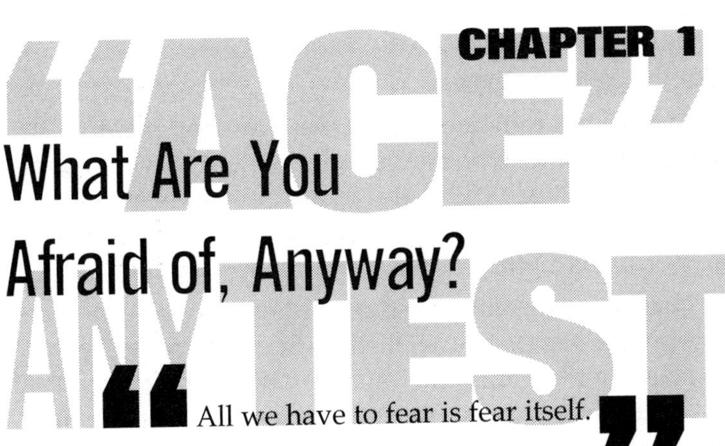

What Are You Afraid of, Anyway?

> "All we have to fear is fear itself."
>
> —Franklin Delano Roosevelt

DR WAS *ALMOST* right. The only thing you *may* have to fear is fear itself. But, frankly, you don't *have* to. You just have to conquer it or beat it into submission so that you can get on with your life—and your biology exam.

But it doesn't hurt to have a little anxiety. You don't want to become so complacent that you lose that edge you need to be truly "up and running" for the test.

Let's spend a few minutes talking about why tests scare people, and then I'll help you learn how to spend your time studying instead of wasting it on anxiety attacks.

The sound of two knees shaking

I still remember a documentary I saw on TV years ago about a famous singer. The camera had been following her around while she went to rehearsal, got her makeup on, and talked with her manager.

The scene I remember most was the shot of her as she waited backstage to be announced, looking nervous, horrified, petrified, regretful that she'd ever entered show business, and extremely vulnerable. (Presuming she remembered she was being filmed, this was the *controlled* panic.)

But when the announcer called her name and the roar of applause began, she walked with a determined gait to the stage, smiled, took the microphone, and never looked back. Her famous voice filled the auditorium, and the audience went wild. If she had those little panics and still passed the test, why shouldn't you?

Speech? Sure, right after I kill myself!

Truly successful entertainers or public speakers will usually admit they get those little knots in their stomachs just before they have to perform. They would be the first ones to tell you that not only is it okay to go through a nervous moment or two, it's actually a benefit, giving them the adrenaline rush they need to do a good job.

Frankly, I usually don't get nervous before a speech or TV appearance—I've just done too many of them—but I will never forget the sweating, slobbering basket case I became when I had to actually stand up and do a book report in 7th grade! Even after thousands of public appearances, there are still times when the old nerve ends tingle a bit while backstage. Know what? I always give a *better* speech.

Let's put that back into the context of your exam-taking: You may have taken a test in the past where you thought you knew everything, did little if any studying—and got a bad grade. Don't go too far the other way.

But don't get too tensed up either. Keep a little anxiety in your life. Just keep it under control and in perspective.

Why is there terror present in the first place? Because we don't want to fail. We realize that, within the next 30 or 60 minutes, a percentage of our grade will be determined by what we write or *don't* write down on a piece of paper or in a blue book, or which box we color in with our No. 2 pencil.

So what are you afraid of?

Now, why do some people fail? What does it mean when someone proclaims they don't "test well"? For many, it really means they don't study well (or, at the very least, prepare well). For others, it could mean they are easily distracted, unprepared for the type of test they are confronting, or simply unprepared mentally to take any test (which may well include mentally sabotaging themselves into a poor score or grade, even though they know the material backwards and forwards).

Take heart—very few people look forward to a test; more of you are afraid of tests than you'd think. But that doesn't mean you *have* to fear them.

We all recognize the competitive nature of tests. Some of us rise to the occasion when facing such a challenge. Others are thrown off balance by the pressure. Both reactions probably have little to do with one's level of knowledge, relative intelligence, or preparation. The smartest students in your class may be the ones most afraid of tests.

Sometimes, it's not fear of failure—it's fear of *success*. You think to yourself, "If I do well on this exam, my parents will expect me to do well on the next exam—and the teacher will think I'm going to do well every day!"

Fear of success gets boring nearly as quickly as would-be martyrs and know-it-all busybodies. Look at it this way: You'll have to deal with some sort of pressure every day of your life. So you might as well learn to handle the *good* kind ("Way to go, genius, keep up the good work!") than the other

("I just don't understand why Tim does so poorly in school. He just doesn't apply himself").

Nobody likes Saralee anyway

Another reason for failure? Some people can't deal with competition. All they can think about is what Saralee is doing. Look at her! She's sitting there, writing down one answer after another—and you know they're all correct!

Who cares about Saralee? I sure wouldn't. Only one person in that room should be concerned with Saralee and Saralee's performance. That's right. Just as only one person should be concerned with *your* performance. Make it all a game: Compete with yourself. See if you can't beat your previous test scores. Now, that's positive competition!

My then 7-year-old daughter, Lindsay, clarified this point when she ran the 100-yard dash for her 1st-grade track team. Despite the fact she was the second fastest of nearly 50 girls, she cried at the end of the race because she wasn't *first.* Is there a little too much pressure here? Can I hear a "Keep it in perspective"? Amen.

You don't have to join the club

Some people thrive on their own misery and are jealous if you don't thrive on it too. They want to include you in all of their hand-wringing situations, regardless of whether you really know or care what's happening. These are people to avoid when you're preparing for an exam—the Anxiety Professionals.

"Oh, I'll never learn all this stuff!" they cry. You might not win points with Miss Manners if you say, "If you'd shut up and study, you might!" You *can* have the pleasure of *thinking* it—on your way to a quiet place to study alone.

Watch out for those "friends" who call you the night before the exam with, "I just found out we have to know Chapter 12!" Don't fall into their trap. Instead of dialing 911, calmly remind them that the printed sheet the professor passed out two weeks ago clearly says that the test will cover chapters 6 through 11. Then hang up, get on with your life, and let them wring their hands all the way to the bottom of the grading sheet. (Of course, if *you* don't bother to check what's going to be on the test, a call like this *will* panic you...and waste your time.)

Focus on the exam

If you have trouble concentrating on your preparations for the exam, try this: Think of your life as a series of shoe boxes (the Imelda Marcos Theory). The boxes are all open and lined up in a nice, long, neat row. In each shoe box is a small part of your life—school, work, romantic interest, hobbies, *ad Florsheim*. Although you have to move little pieces from one box to another from time to time, you can—and should—keep this stuff as separate as possible.

Of course, you *can* make it easier to do this by *not* going out of your way—certainly before an especially big or important test—to add *more* stress to an already stressful life. Two days before the SAT is *not* the time to dump a boyfriend, move, change jobs, take out a big loan, or create any other waves in your normally placid river of life.

You're already an expert

For years you've taken pop quizzes, oral exams, standardized tests, and tests on chapters, units, whole books, and whole semesters. For the most part, you've been successful. If you haven't been as successful as you'd like, keep reading. For the remainder of this book, we'll review what you can do to change all that. All this experience, coupled with the real-life "tests" I've already mentioned, demonstrates that you're pretty good—even excellent. Stop for a moment and pat yourself on the back. You are a successful test-taker, in spite of a little fright here and there.

One in a million

Just admitting that you're not at ground zero can help you realize that preparing for an exam is not in itself a whole new task of life—it's merely part of a continuum.

Think of this fraction: one over one million. Your life is the big number. Your next test is the little number. All the "ones" in your life add up to the one million; they are important, but all by themselves, they can't compare to the Giant Economy Number of Life. Write "1/1,000,000" at the top of your next test to remind yourself of that. That alone should kill off a bunch of stomach butterflies.

"Extra" tests give extra help

If you want to practice the many recommendations you're going to get in this book, including what I'm sharing with you in this important first chapter, take a few "extra" tests just to give yourself some practice. It will also help you overcome unacceptable levels of test anxiety.

Get permission from your teachers to retake some old tests to practice test-taking techniques and exorcise the High-Anxiety Demon. Many teachers keep old tests (as well as lecture notes and sample papers) in the school's library. Take a couple of standardized tests that your counseling office might have, too, since the color-in-the-box answer sheets and questions in printed form have their own set of rules (which, you guessed it, we'll talk about later in this book).

A little perspective, please

The more pressure you put on yourself—the larger you allow a test (and, of course, your hoped-for good scores) to loom in your own mind—the less you are helping yourself. Of course, the bigger the test really *is*, the more likely you are to keep reminding yourself of its importance.

No matter how important a test really may be to your career—and your scores on some *can* have a major effect on where you go to college, whether you go to graduate school, whether you get the job you want—it is just as important to *de-emphasize* that test's importance in your mind. This should have no effect on your preparation—you should still study as if your life depended on a superior score. It might!

A friend of mine signed up to take the Law School Admission Test (LSAT), not just once, but twice. The first time, he did "okay, not great." By the time the second date rolled around, he had decided not to become a lawyer. But since he had already paid for the thing, he took the LSAT again anyway. Are you already ahead of me? That's right—a 15-percent improvement with *no* studying. Does that tell you something about trying to downplay all this self-inflicted pressure?

Keeping the whole experience in perspective might also help: Twenty years from now, nobody will remember, or care, what you scored on *any* test—no matter how life-threatening or life-determining you feel that test is now.

Don't underestimate positive thinking: Thoughts *can* become self-fulfilling prophecies. If you tell yourself often enough, "Be careful, you'll fall over that step," you probably will. If you tell yourself often enough, "I'm going to fail this test," you just might. Likewise, keep convincing yourself that you are as prepared as anyone and are going to "ace" the sucker, and you're already ahead of the game.

How to lower your AQ (Anxiety Quotient)

To come to terms with the "importance" of a test, read the following list. Knowing the answers to as many of these questions as possible will help reduce your anxiety.

1. What material will the exam cover?
2. How many total points are possible?
3. What percentage of my semester grade is based on this exam?
4. How much time will I have to take the exam?
5. Where will the exam be held?
6. What kinds of questions will be on the exam (matching, multiple choice, essay, true/false, and so forth)?
7. How many points will be assigned to each question? Will certain types of questions count more than others? How many of each type of question will be on the exam?
8. Will it be an open-book exam?
9. What can I take in with me? Calculator? Candy bar? Other materials crucial to my success?
10. Will I be penalized for wrong answers?

Take a hike, buddy

Finally, to shake off pretest anxiety, take a walk. Or a vigorous swim. In the days before an exam, no matter how "big" it is, don't study too hard or too much or you'll walk into the exam with a fried brain.

Please don't think that advice loses its power at the classroom door. Scheduling breaks during tests has the same effect. During a one-hour test, you may not have time to go out for a stroll. But during a two- or three-hour final, there's no reason you should not schedule one, two, or even more breaks on a periodic basis—whenever you feel you need them most. Such time-outs can consist of a bathroom stop, a quick walk up and down the hall, or just a minute of relaxation in your seat before you continue the test.

No matter what the time limits or pressures, don't feel you cannot afford such a brief respite. You may need it *most* when you're convinced you can *least* afford it, just as those who most need time-management techniques "just don't have the time" to learn them.

Relax, darn it!

If your mind is a jumble of facts and figures, names and dates, you may find it difficult to zero in on the specific details you need to recall, even if you know all the material backwards and forwards. The adrenaline rushing through your system may make "instant retrieval" seem impossible.

The simplest relaxation technique is deep breathing. Just lean back in your chair, relax your muscles, and take three very deep breaths (count to 10 while you hold each one). For many of you, that's the only relaxation technique you'll ever need.

There are a variety of meditation techniques that may also work for you. Each is based upon a similar principle—focusing your mind on one thing to the exclusion of everything else. While you're concentrating on the object of your meditation (even if the object is nothing, a nonsense word, or a spot on the wall,) your mind can't be thinking about anything else, which allows it to slow down a bit.

Whichever technique you feel you need to use, remember this important fact: The more you believe in the technique, the more it will work. Just like your belief that you're going to "ace" that test!

CHAPTER 2

Creating the Time to Study

> "Work expands so as to fill the time available for its completion."
>
> –Cyril Parkinson, *Parkinson's Law*

> "I recommend that you learn to take care of the minutes, for the hours will take care of themselves."
>
> —Lord Chesterfield

POOR TIME. IT really gets a bum rap. We all have problems with it. We can't slow it down, speed it up, or save it up—all we can do is decide how we're going to spend it. We invariably need more of it...and don't know where to find it. Then we wonder where the heck it all went.

But time isn't really the problem. We all get 24 hours, same for you, me, and Saralee. The problem is that most of us have never been taught how to manage our time...or why we should even try. Our parents never sat us down to give us a little "facts of time" talk, and time-management skills aren't part of any standard academic curriculum.

Not knowing how to effectively manage our time, we just continue to use the "natural" approach, simply taking things as they come and doing what we feel like doing, without schedule or plan. What the heck—it worked when we were kids. It was easy to live from day to day and never really worry about where our time went.

In fact, sometimes there seemed to be too *much* time—too many *hours* before school was over...too many *days* before summer vacation...too many *weeks* before birthdays... too many *years* before we could learn to drive.

Unfortunately for all of us Peter Pans, there comes a point—too soon, perhaps—when the take-every-day-as-it-comes approach just doesn't work. For most of us, it hits in high school. (If you're in high school and don't know what I'm talking about, don't worry—you'll find out in college.) Why? Because that's when we begin to establish goals that are important to *us,* not just to our parents.

To achieve our goals, we must commit ourselves to the many and varied steps it takes to get there. We must plan. We must *manage* our time.

Whether you're a high school student just starting to feel frazzled; a college student juggling five classes and a part-time job; or a parent working, attending classes, and raising a family, a simple, easy-to-follow time-management system is crucial to your success. Despite your natural tendency to proclaim that you just don't have the *time* to spend scheduling, listing, and recording, it's also the best way to give yourself *more* time.

So, let's start by making a major adjustment in our thinking: Time is our *friend,* not our enemy. Time allows us space in each day or week or month to do a lot of fun things and to reach certain milestones in order to advance our careers, get diplomas or degrees, establish and develop relationships, go on vacations, and all that good stuff.

It also allows us to prepare for tests. (Let's not get carried away and forget the focus of this book.) This chapter includes some simple time charts that will help you work on *when, where,* and *how* you manage the various demands on your time.

Look at it this way: Between now and next Tuesday, whether you are preparing to play in the state basketball tournament, writing a paper about the Mississippi Delta, or holding down three jobs (or, heaven help you, all of the above), you have exactly the same amount of time as the rest of us. It's what you *do* with that time that makes the difference.

How are you going to get from here to there? Are you just going to go crashing along, like an elephant trampling down banana trees, or are you going to get there by following a plan? Good. That's the right answer. See? You just passed *another* test. Congratulations.

You spend three hours a day resting?

The first step to overhauling your current routine is to identify that routine, in detail. My suggestion is to chart, in 15-minute increments, how you spend every minute of every day, *right now*. While a day or two might be sufficient for some of you, I recommend you chart your activities for an entire week, including the weekend.

This is especially important if, like many people, you have huge pockets of time that seemingly disappear, but, in reality, are devoted to things like "resting" after you wake up, putting on makeup and shaving, reading the paper, waiting for transportation, or driving to and from school or work. Could you use an extra hour or two a day, either for studying or for fun? Make better use of such "dead" time and you may well find the time you need.

For example, learn how to do multiple tasks at the same time. Listen to a book on tape while you're working around the house; practice vocabulary or math drills while you're driving; have your kids, parents, or roommates quiz you for an upcoming test while you're doing the dishes, vacuuming, or dusting. *Always* carry your calendar, notebook(s), pens, and a textbook with you—you can get a phenomenal amount of reading or studying done while in line at the bank, in the library, at the supermarket, or on a bus or train.

The more willing you are to transform "dead" time into study time, the more ways you'll invent to do so.

Set up a "future" drawer in your filing cabinet. When you find ideas, research material, and so forth (from magazines, books, newspapers, Web sites, whatever) that you think may be important *sometime in the future,* write a pertinent note to yourself and file it. The time you take now will be a mere fraction of the time you save in the future.

If you can afford it, take advantage of technology's efficiencies. For example, you can now buy a combination printer, fax, scanner, and copier for less than $500. Doesn't that beat paying a typist and donating quarters to the photocopier at the library?

Focus = efficiency

How often have you made a "to-do" list and then either forgotten it, lost it, or ignored it? To-do lists have incredible merits, but they're not much good if you don't use them. You can't effectively deal with *today's* priorities if you still have to contend with yesterday's...or last week's!

Let's run through the composition and execution of a to-do list for a shopping expedition as an example. Here's what I do when I am making up a list of errands.

First, after writing down where I have to go, I turn the paper over and make individual lists of items for each stopping place. I may have Smith's drug store on the "where to go" front side of the list, but on the back I have listed shaving cream, bubble gum, newspaper, hair spray, and prescriptions.

Am I (A) obsessive-compulsive or (B) merely organized? If this were a real test, the correct answer would be (B).

By separating the *where* from the *what*, I am able to focus on getting from the post office to the drug store to the hardware store without trying to separate the stamps from the toothpaste from the tool kit. On the other hand, when I am heading down Aisle 3B, I can concentrate on what items I need from this particular stop.

I do one more thing on my shopping list: If I need to take anything with me (return a video, drop off my cleaning, take an article to be photocopied), I place a "T" (meaning "take") with a circle around it beside the place for which I need the "T" item. That way, I don't get to Smith's only to discover that I forgot to bring the prescription form. (If it's convenient, put all the "T" items, along with the list, beside the door so you won't have to search for them when it's time to leave.)

Now, why am I sharing all this detailed information on my shopping-list habits when we're supposed to be talking about getting ready for your zoology exam? Because the methods and the rationale are similar to your management of time. Here's what my list does for me:

- I don't forget anything.
- I save time.
- I get things done easily.
- I "save" my brain for what's important.

Attention, Study-Smart shoppers!

Think of the time between now and your next exam as your shopping trip. You want to use this time most effectively so that (1) you don't forget anything, (2) you work efficiently (save time), (3) you arrange your studying so it's done as easily as possible, and (4) you concentrate on the important details, not on *all* the details (big difference!).

How much time do you have? Unless I missed something in the paper this morning, we all have 24 hours a day. But you and I know that's not what we're talking about here. We have to subtract sleeping, eating, commuting, and obligations like work and classes...whoa! Any time left?

Sure there is. But first you need to get a handle on what you *must* do, what you *should* do, and what you *want* to do. Let's refer to them as our H, M, and L priorities.

The H (high) priorities are those things we *must* do between now and the next test.

The M (medium) priorities are those things we *should* do, but we could postpone without being jailed or written out of the will.

The L (low) priorities are those things we want to do but that are *expendable.* At least until you have finished taking this next exam.

Remember to break any long-term or difficult projects into small, "bite-size" tasks that can be included on your schedule. As Henry Ford said, "Nothing is particularly hard if you divide it into small jobs." Hence, the assembly line.

Time-saving tip: If you push aside the same low-priority item day after day, week after week, at some point you should just stop and decide whether it's something you need to do at all! This is a strategic way to make a task or problem "disappear."

Yes, Virginia, it's all right to sleep

An "H" is sleeping, eating, and attending class—especially the class in question. You simply can't ignore these.

An "M" is getting your family car's oil changed or taking your cat to the vet for a checkup. Important, but unless the car's dipstick shows that it has no oil or the cat is so sick it's trying to dial the vet's number itself, these tasks can be delayed for a handful of days.

An "L" is going to the Hitchcock Film Festival or partying with friends up at the cabin in the mountains.

In ***Get Organized,*** I give you three different forms to use. I'm including them in this book as well. The first one, the Term Planning Calendar, helps you sort out and manage the big picture. The second, Priority Tasks This Week, breaks the semester down into seven-day periods. The third, Daily Schedule, will reduce it to a focused day-by-day format.

Let's talk about the Term Planning Calendar on page 32. Simply put, this is a series of monthly calendars with all the important events listed on them. Sounds pretty simple. Actually, it is. Even if you've only got six weeks left in the semester, go ahead and fill out one of these.

Don't just list school-related items ("Biology semester exam, 9 a.m." on May 3); put down the "H" items from the rest of your life, too ("Trip to Chicago" on March 22).

One very good reason for listing all the social/personal/nonacademic items is for you to determine which of those are going to remain in the "H" category. For example, if you discover that you have planned a trip to Chicago for the weekend before your French midterm the following Monday, you'd better cry *"Sacre bleu!"* and decide the Chicago trip is an "L" and must be moved to another weekend.

Get the picture?

One of the most important reasons for writing down what exactly is coming up is to get that big picture. Once you've filled in all the due dates of term papers, unit tests, midterms, finals, project reports, and so forth, take a good look at the results.

Are there a bunch of deadlines in the same week or even on the same day? During finals and midterms, of course, this really can't be helped because there's no way to take the tests at another time.

TERM PLANNING CALENDAR

Fill in due dates for assignments and papers, dates of tests, and important non-academic activities and events.

Month	MON	TUE	WED	THU	FRI	SAT	SUN

Perhaps you can do something about some of the other deadlines. If you have a French test covering three units on the same day that you have to turn in a paper on the "Influence of the Beatles on British Foreign Policy" and a status report on your gerbil project for sociology, take the plunge and decide that you will get the paper and the project status report done early so that you can devote the time just prior to that day to studying for your French test.

You can't make decisions like that, however, if you can't sit back and get an overall view. I like to sit back literally and look at the Term Planning Calendar so I can easily see where several deadlines are on the same day or week.

Looking at everything that is coming up will help you decide what is really an "H" and what is not. It need not cut into your social life, but it does mean that you may need to rearrange some things or say no to some invitations that come smack in the middle of your gathering data on gerbils.

But you can have fun and frolic on the nights and weekends that are far enough away from your "H" priorities. When personal "H" events come up (you really can't miss your sister's wedding, no matter how much the gerbils need you), your Term Planning Calendar gives you enough warning so that you can make sure your schoolwork doesn't suffer.

"I should have planned better"

Once you have a grasp of your obligations for a term at a time, bring the tasks down to the week at hand by filling out the Priority Tasks This Week form (see the sample on page 34, which you can photocopy and use). When planning study time for a test during the week, find the answers to these two questions: (1) How much time do I *need* to devote to studying for this exam? and (2) How much time do I *have* to study for this exam?

Priority Rating	Scheduled?	PRIORITY TASKS THIS WEEK Week of ______ through ______

It's fairly easy to determine the answer to the second question. After all, there are a finite number of hours between now and the exam, and you are filling in the "H" priorities and figuring that a certain amount of time devoted to sleeping and eating is necessary.

But the first question calls for a fairly definitive answer, too, or else you will never be able to plan.

Consider these other questions when figuring out the time needed:

- How much time do I usually spend studying for this type of exam? Have the results been successful?
- What grade do I have going for me now? (If it's a solid B and you're convinced you can't get an A, you may decide to devote less time to studying for the exam.)
- What special studying do I have to do?
- Organize the materials you need to study, pace yourself, and check to see how much material you have covered in the first hour of review. How does this compare to what you have left to study?

Be careful how you "divvy up" your valuable study time. Schedule enough time for the task, but not so much time that you burn out. Every individual is different, but most students study best for blocks of about one and a half to three hours, depending on the subject. You might find history fascinating and be able to read for hours. Calculus, on the other hand, may be a subject that you can best handle in small bites, a half-hour to an hour at a time.

Don't overdo it. Plan your study time in blocks, breaking up work time with short leisure activities. It's helpful to add these to your schedule as well. You'll find that these breaks help you think more clearly and creatively when you get back to studying.

Even if you tend to like longer blocks of study time, be careful about scheduling study marathons—six- or eight-hour stretches rather than a series of two-hour sessions. The longer the period you schedule, the more likely you'll have to fight the demons of procrastination. Convincing yourself that you are really studying your heart out, you'll also find it easier to justify time-wasting distractions, scheduling longer breaks, and, before long, quitting before you should.

If you find yourself fighting this demon, remind yourself (frequently) of the Law of Diminishing Returns: Your initial effort yields the biggest results, with each succeeding effort yielding proportionately less. And there comes a point where even the most *prodigious* efforts yield *negligible* results. This applies not only to perfectionists, but also to those of you who scoff at the very thought of using a "simple" outline or producing a "formulaic" report. You do not have to always be innovative, dazzling, and creative or add yet another hour of study time to the days you've already allocated to finals. Have you ever heard of an athlete who "leaves it on the practice court?" That means he is a killer during practice and a washout during games. Don't leave *your* game on the practice court by *over*preparing.

When I am tempted to do far more than necessary, just because it would be a "cool" solution (and time-consuming and wasteful and inefficient and difficult), I think of George Simenon, the French author best known for his Inspector Maigret mystery series—and the *500 total books he wrote* in his lifetime. How did he do it...and still have time to eat and sleep? Simple. He used only 2,000 vocabulary words (out of the 800,000 plus available to him) so he wouldn't have to interrupt his writing to consult a dictionary or thesaurus. (And he probably didn't eat or sleep much, either.)

Listen to the chimes of your unique "study clock": Schedule the easiest tasks during nonprime hours. When your energy and motivation are at their lowest levels, should you really bore in on that project that's been giving you fits? Or merely recopy some notes, go over your calendar, or proofread a paper? When you're least creative, least energetic, and least motivated, why would you even consider tackling your most challenging assignments? Don't be like many businesspeople I know who schedule their time "bass-ackwards": In the morning, when they're raring to go, they read the paper, check their e-mail, and skim trade journals. At the *end* of the day, when they can barely see straight, they start on the presentation for the Board of Directors' meeting...*tomorrow's* Board of Directors' meeting.

Don't be dazed

Now we get to the Daily Schedule (see the sample on page 38, which you can photocopy and use), the piece of paper that will keep you sane as you move through the day.

Your Term Planning Calendar will most likely be on the wall beside your study area in your dorm, apartment, or house. Your Priority Tasks This Week should be carried with you so that you can add any items that suddenly come up in class ("Oh," your teacher says, "did I forget to tell you that we have a quiz on Friday on the first two chapters?") or in conversation ("Go skiing with you this weekend? With you *and* your gorgeous twin? Let me check my calendar!").

Carry your Daily Schedule so that you can be sure not to forget *anything*. The Daily Schedule, by the way, is divided into four categories:

1. **Assignments due.** What has to be turned in on this day. Check before you leave for class. (This is like the "T" notation on my shopping list.)

DAILY SCHEDULE

Date:

Assignments Due

To Do/Errands

Homework

Schedule
5
6
7
8
9
10
11
12
1
2
3
4
5
6
7
8
9
10
11
12

2. **To do/errands.** Don't depend on your memory. It's not that you can't remember; it's that you don't need to remember. This column will help you plan ahead (for example, actually buying a birthday present before the birthday) and save you last-minute panic when you should be studying for the upcoming exam.
3. **Homework.** When the teacher gives out homework assignments, here's where you can write them down so they're all together, complete with due dates, page numbers, and any other information from the teacher.
4. **Schedule.** The actual list of events for the day from early morning to late night. This is especially important when you have something extraordinary happening.

In fact, you should highlight any unusual happenings with a bright-colored pen just to remind yourself. Take a moment to glance over the day's schedule *twice*: Look at it the night before, to psych yourself up for the coming day and make sure you didn't forget to do any special assignments. Then, glance at it again while you're having a quiet moment during your nutritious breakfast that morning.

Using these time-saving tools effectively

Organizing your life requires you to actually *use* these tools. Once you have discovered habits and patterns of study that work for you, continue to use and hone them.

When you're scheduling your time, be specific about which tasks you plan to do and when you plan to do them.

Don't delay your planning. It's easy to convince yourself that you will plan the details of a particular task when the time comes. You may tell yourself, "I'll just leave my schedule blank and plan the afternoon right after I get out of biology." But that way it's much too easy to forget your homework when your friends invite you to go to the park or out for a snack.

Plan according to *your* schedule, *your* goals, and *your* aptitudes, not some ephemeral "standard." Allocate the time you expect a project to take *you*, not the time it might take someone else, how long your teacher says it should take, and so forth. Try to be realistic and honest with yourself when determining those things that require more effort or those that come easier to you.

Whenever possible, schedule pleasurable activities *after* study time, not before. They will then act as incentives, not distractions.

Be flexible and ready. Changes happen and you'll have to adjust your schedule to accommodate them.

Monitor your progress at reasonable periods and make changes where necessary. Remember, this is *your* study regimen—you conceived it, you can change it.

If you find that you are consistently allotting more time than necessary to a particular chore—say, giving yourself an hour to review your English notes every Sunday but always finishing in 45 minutes or less—change your future schedule accordingly.

As assignments are entered on your calendar, make sure you also enter items needed—texts; other books you have to buy, borrow, or get from the library; and special materials such as drawing pads, magic markers, graph paper, and so on.

Adapt these tools for your own use. Try anything you think may work—use it if it does, discard it if it doesn't.

Do your least favorite chores (study assignments, projects, whatever) first—you'll feel better having gotten them out of the way! Plan how to accomplish them as meticulously as possible. That will get rid of them even faster.

Accomplish one task before going on to the next one—don't skip around. If you see that you are moving along faster than you anticipated on one task or project sequence, there is absolutely nothing wrong with continuing onto the next part of that assignment or the next project step.

If you are behind, don't panic. Just take the time to reorganize your schedule and find the time you need to make up. You may be able to free up time from another task or put one part of a long-term project off for a day or two.

The tools we've discussed and the various other hints should get you into the habit of writing things down. Not having to remember all these items will free up space in your brain for the things you need to concentrate on or *do* have to remember.

Learn to manage distractions. As a time-management axiom puts it, "Don't respond to the urgent and forget the important." Some things you do can be picked up or dropped at any time. Beware of these time-consuming and complicated tasks that, once begun, demand to be completed. Interrupting at any point might mean starting all over again. What a waste of time *that* would be!

Nothing can be as counterproductive as losing your concentration, especially at critical times. Learn to ward off those enemies that would alter your course and you will find your journey much smoother.

One way to guard against mental intrusions is to know your own study clock and plan your study time accordingly. Each of us is predisposed to function most efficiently at specific times of day (or night). Find out what sort of clock you're on and schedule your work during this period.

Beware of uninvited guests and *all* phone calls: Unless you are ready for a break, they'll only get you off schedule. More subtle enemies include the sudden desire to sharpen every pencil in the house, an unheard-of urge to clean your room, an offer to do your sister's homework. Anything, in other words, to avoid your own work.

Saying no (to others or yourself) will help insulate yourself from these unnecessary (and postponable) interruptions. Put up your "Do Not Disturb" sign and stick to your guns, no matter what the temptation.

Time is relative. Car trips take longer if you have to schedule frequent stops for gas, food, and so on, longer still if you start out during rush hour. So take the time of day into account. If your schedule involves working with others, take *their* sense of time into account—you may have to schedule "waiting time" for a chronically late friend...and always bring a book along.

Going into "test training"

If you have an upcoming exam early in the morning and you are afraid you won't be in shape for it, do a bit of subterfuge on your body and brain.

Get up early for several days before the exam, have a good breakfast, and do homework or review your notes. This will help jump-start your body and brain and get used to the idea of having to solve equations or think seriously about the Punjab at an earlier-than-usual hour.

At the other end of the day, take care to get to bed early enough. Forego the late-night parties and the midnight movie on TV and actually devote enough time to getting some serious ZZZZZs.

Cramming doesn't work

In case I didn't mention it yet, *cramming does not work.* We've all done it at one time or another, with one excuse or another—waited until the last minute and then tried to fit a week's, month's, or entire semester's worth of work into a single night or weekend. Did it work? Doubt it.

After a night of no sleep and too much coffee, most of us are lucky if we remember where the test *is* the next day. A few hours later, trying to stay awake long enough to make it back to bed, we not only haven't learned anything, we haven't done well on the test we crammed for!

How to cram anyway

Nevertheless, despite your resolve, best intentions, and firm conviction that cramming is a losing proposition, you may well find yourself—though hopefully not too often—in the position of needing to do *some*thing the night before a test you haven't studied for at all. If so, there are some rules to follow that will make your night of cramming at least marginally successful.

Be realistic about what you can do. You absolutely *cannot* master a semester's worth of work in one night. The *more* you try to cram in, the *less* effective you will be.

Be selective and study in depth. The more you've missed, the more selective you must be in organizing your cram session. You *can't* study it all.

Massage your memory. Use every memory technique you know (and those in ***Improve Your Memory***) to maximize what you can retain in your short-term memory.

Know when to give up. When you can't remember your name or see the page in front of you, get some sleep.

Consider an early-morning versus a late-night cram. Especially if you're a morning person, but even if you're not, I've found it more effective to go to bed and get up early rather than go to bed late and get up exhausted.

Spend the first few minutes writing down whatever you remember now but are afraid you'll forget, especially when your mind is trying to hold on to so many facts and figures it seems ready to explode.

Get a copy of another of my books—*Last Minute Study Tips.* It will help you prepare for a test that's weeks, days, hours, or just minutes away...and do better on it.

Studying with kids

Since many of you are going to school while raising a family, I want to add some particular tidbits of advice for studying with screaming munchkins gnawing at your legs:

Plan activities to keep the kids occupied. The busier you are in school or at work, the more time your kids will want from you when you *are* home. If you spend a little time with them, it may be easier for them to play alone, especially if you've created projects *they* can work on while *you're* working on your homework.

Make the kids part of your study routine. Kids love routine, so include them in yours. If 5:30 to 7:30 is "Dad's Study Time," they'll get used to it, especially if you make spending other time with them a priority and give them something to do during those hours.

Use the television as a babysitter. While many of you disapprove of this, it may be the lesser of two evils.

Plan your study accordingly. Take more frequent breaks to spend five minutes with your kids. They'll be more likely to give you the 15 or 20 minutes at a time *you* need if they get periodic attention themselves.

Find help. Spouses can occasionally take the kids out for dinner and a movie, relatives can babysit at their homes on a rotating basis, playmates can be invited over (allowing you to send your darling to their house the next day), you may be able to trade babysitting chores with other parents at school, and professional daycare may be available at your child's school or in someone's home for a few hours a day. Be creative in finding the help you need.

CHAPTER 3

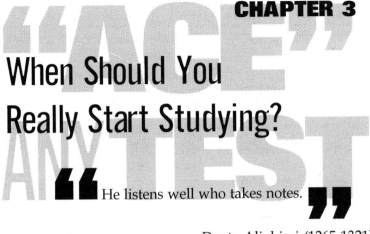

When Should You Really Start Studying?

> He listens well who takes notes. 
>
> —Dante Alighieri (1265-1321)

ONCE UPON A time, there was a very hard-working student named Melvin. He read his textbooks, took good notes in class, rarely missed a day of school, and always did his homework. Sitting next to him in class was a guy named Steve. This guy *sort of* took notes, *kind of* read his textbook, and *usually* did his homework. Well, okay, not usually, but *kind of* usually—if he came to class at all.

The day of the big test came. Hard-working Melvin got a D and slouchy, lazy Steve got an A.

If you believe this bears any resemblance to reality, please read and reread every one of the books in my ***How to Study Program***. You need all the help you can get.

The first day of the test of your life

Well, maybe I shouldn't really say "test of your life." It sounds as if you may not come out of this one alive. Even the SAT isn't that important or scary!

What I really want to emphasize in this chapter was hinted at in the "once upon a time" story on the previous page: You don't start preparing for a test a couple of days before. You begin when you walk into the classroom on the first day—or even *before* that.

Too many students think the exam is out there all by itself—floating out in space like a balloon that got loose from a bawling toddler at a carnival. Nope.

Everything you do in that course—attending every class, applying listening skills, taking good notes, doing your homework, and reading all the assignments—helps you in "studying" for the exam.

For whom the alarm clock tolls

Yes, my friend, it may be cruel and it may be cold, but getting out of bed and going to class is the first step toward passing the final that's four months away.

"Missing that biology class just this one time can't huuuuurrrrrt!" you moan as you roll over and bury your head under the pillow.

Obviously, if this is you, you've got to start by getting to bed a little bit earlier, planning ahead a little bit more, and deciding that going to class is something you must do automatically.

Now that you're here...

All right. I got you out of bed and inside the classroom. You're awake, polite, respectful, and listening. Now what?

Actually, that question should have been asked last night or several nights ago. You can't just waltz into class and be up to speed. When you arrive, your teacher expects you to have:

1. Read the assignment.
2. Brought your notes/textbooks.
3. Brought your homework assignment.
4. Opened your notebook to the right page, opened the textbook to the current chapter, and taken out your homework to hand it in.

Pop goes the quiz

Not all tests, as you know by now, are announced. Your teacher may decide, out of malice, boredom, or his lesson-plan book, to give you a pop quiz.

Now, how can you score well if you, first of all, aren't in class and, second of all, haven't read the new material and periodically reviewed the old? And suppose it's an open-book test and you don't have a book to open?

Let's face it. Biology, U.S. history, economics, or whatever 101 may not be your favorite subject, but that doesn't mean you have to have an attitude about it. "Proving" you can't or won't do well in a class proves nothing.

The next steps

Let's move on to what you should do during class, after class, and before class.

Taking effective notes during class requires five separate actions on your part:

1. *Listening* actively;
2. *Selecting* pertinent information;
3. *Condensing* it;

4. *Sorting*/organizing it;
5. *Interpreting* it (later).

So, during class, you need to listen and observe. Not a difficult task, even when the teacher isn't going to win any elocution or acting awards. Identifying noteworthy material means finding a way to separate the wheat—that which you *should* write down—from the chaff—that which you should *ignore*.

How do you do that? By *listening* for verbal clues and *watching* for nonverbal ones.

Many teachers will invariably signal important material in the way they present it—pausing (waiting for all the pens to rise), repeating the same point (perhaps even one already made and repeated in your textbook), slowing down their normally supersonic lecture speed, speaking more loudly (or more softly), or even by simply stating, "I think the following is important."

There are also a number of words and phrases that should *signal* noteworthy material (and, at the same time, give you the clues you need to organize your notes logically): "first of all," "most importantly," "therefore," "as a result," "to summarize," "on the other hand," "on the contrary," "the following (number of) reasons (causes, effects, decisions, facts, and so forth)."

Words and phrases such as these give you the clues to not just write down the lecture material that follows but to put it in context—to make a list ("first," "the following reasons"); establish a cause-and-effect relationship ("therefore," "as a result"); establish opposites or alternatives ("on the other hand," "on the contrary," "alternatively"); signify a conclusion ("therefore," "to summarize"); or offer an explanation or definition.

Don't just listen, watch!

If the teacher begins looking at the window, or his eyes glaze over, he's sending you a clear signal: "This isn't going to be on the test." (So don't take notes!)

On the other hand, if she turns to write something on the blackboard, makes eye contact with several students, and/or gestures dramatically, she's sending a clear signal about the importance of the point she's making.

Of course, there are many exceptions to this rule. My first-year calculus instructor would occasionally launch into long diatribes about his mother or air pollution, in tones more impassioned than any he ever used working through differential equations.

There was also the trigonometry professor I endured who got all worked up about the damage being done to the nation's sidewalks by the deadly menace of chewing gum.

Nevertheless, be a detective—don't overlook the clues.

You are your own best note-taker

I'm sure you've observed in your classes that some people are constantly taking notes. Others end up with two lines on one page. Most of us fall in between.

The person who never stops taking notes is either writing a letter to a friend in Iowa or has absolutely no idea what *is* or is *not* important.

The results are dozens of pages of notes (by the end of the semester) that may or may not be helpful. This person is so busy writing down stuff that he isn't prepared or even aware that he can ask and answer questions to help him understand the material better. To use that old adage, he can't see the forest for the trees. He is probably the same person who takes a marking pen and underlines or highlights every word in the book.

Contrast him to the guy who thinks note-taking isn't cool, so he only writes down today's date and the homework assignment. He may write something when the teacher says, "Now, write this down and remember it," but he probably just scribbles some nonsense words. After all, he's cool.

Watch him sweat when it's time to study for the exam. He's stuck with a faulty memory and a textbook that may not contain half the material that will be on the test.

Take notes on what you don't know

You *know* the first lines of Hamlet's soliloquy. You *know* the chemical formula for salt. You *know* the date Nixon resigned. So why waste time and space writing them down?

Frequently, your teachers will present material you already know in order to set the stage for further discussion, or to introduce material that is more difficult. Don't be so conditioned to automatically copy down dates, vocabulary, terms, formulas, and names that you mindlessly take notes on information you already know. You'll just be wasting your time—both in class and later, when you review your overly detailed notes.

Items discussed during any lesson could be grouped into several categories, which vary in importance:

- ✎ **Information** not contained in the class texts and other assigned readings.
- ✎ **Explanations** of obscure material covered in the texts and readings but with which students might have difficulty.
- ✎ **Demonstrations or examples** that provided greater understanding of the subject matter.
- ✎ **Background information** that put the course material in context.

As you are listening to an instructor, decide which of these categories best fits the information being presented. This will help you determine how detailed your notes on the material should be. (This will become especially easy as you get to know the instructor.)

Notes: Tools of the trade

For a time, I found it very useful to type my notes after I'd written them in class. First of all, my handwriting won't win any prizes. I noticed early on that very few people asked to borrow my notes. "Is this word 'Madagascar' or 'Muncie'?" they'd ask a little too loudly.

Second, typing the notes gave me an opportunity to have a quick review of the class, spell out most of my abbreviations, and—most importantly—discover if I missed anything.

A neater version of my notes was also extremely helpful when it came time to study for the test. I could read what was there, I had highlighted the most important elements, and the whole batch of notes just made more sense.

Why did I say I did this "for a time"? Because I stopped doing it my second year of college and haven't done it since. Instead, I concentrated on developing my own shorthand system that minimized the need to rewrite anything and maximized my ability to capture "noteworthy" materials the first (and only) time around.

Looks aren't everything, but...

You'll want your class notes to be as readable and "studyable" as possible.

You don't have to be a master of shorthand to streamline your note-taking. Here are five ways:

1. **Eliminate vowels.** As a sign that was ubiquitous in the New York City subways used to proclaim, "If u cn rd ths, u cn gt a gd jb." ("If you can read this, you can get a good job.")
2. **Use word beginnings** ("rep" for representative, "con" for Congressperson), and other easy-to-remember abbreviations.
3. **Stop putting periods** after all abbreviations (they add up!).
4. **Use standard symbols** in place of words. The list on page 53 will help you out in most of your classes (you may recognize many of these symbols from math and logic).
5. **Create your own symbols and abbreviations** based on your needs and comfort level.

   There are three symbols I think you'll want to create—they'll be needed again and again.

   Ⓦ That's my symbol for "what?" as in "What the heck does that mean?"; "What did she say?"; or "What happened? I'm completely lost!" It denotes something that's been missed—leave space in your notes to fill in the missing part of the puzzle after class.

   Ⓜ That's my symbol for "my thought." I want to separate my thoughts during a lecture from the professor's.

   (T!) My symbol for "test!" as in "He actually *said* this is going to be on the test!"

Feel free to use your own code for these three instances; you certainly don't have to use mine. While I recommend using all the "common" symbols and abbreviations listed previously *all* the time, in *every* class, in order to maintain consistency, you may want to create specific symbols or abbreviations for each class. In chemistry, "TD" may stand for

Standard shorthand symbols	
≈	approximately
w/	with
w/o	without
wh/	which
→	resulting in
←	as a result of/consequence of
+	and or also
*	most importantly
cf	compare; in comparison; in relation to
ff	following
<	less than
>	more than
=	the same as
↑	increasing
↓	decreasing
esp	especially
Δ	change
⊂	it follows that
∴	therefore
b/c	because

thermodynamics, and "K" for the Kinetic Theory of Gasses (but don't confuse it with "Kelvin"). In history, "GW" is the father of our country, "ABE" is Mr. Honesty, "FR" could be French Revolution (or "freedom rider"), and "IR" is Industrial Revolution.

To tape or not to tape

I am opposed to using a tape recorder in class as a substitute for an active brain for the following reasons:

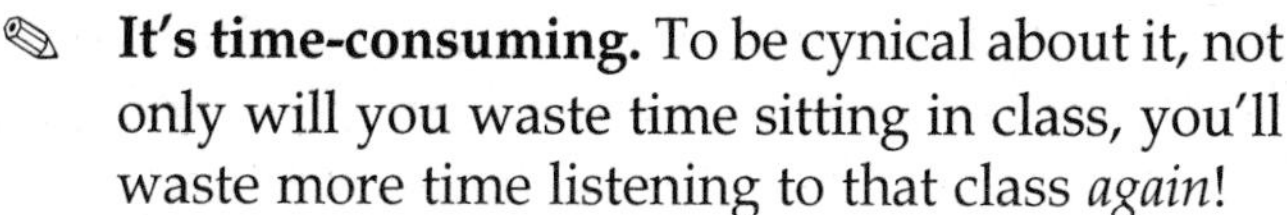

✎ **It's time-consuming.** To be cynical about it, not only will you waste time sitting in class, you'll waste more time listening to that class *again*!

- **It's virtually useless for review.** During the hectic days before an exam, do you really want to waste time listening to a whole lecture when you could just reread your notes?
- **It offers no backup.** Only the most diligent students will record *and* take notes. But what happens if your tape recorder malfunctions? How useful will blank or distorted tapes be to you when it's time to review? If you're going to take notes as a backup, why not just take good notes and leave the tape recorder home?
- **It costs money.** Compare the price of paper and a pen to that of recorder, batteries, and tapes. The cost of batteries *alone* should convince you that you're better off going the low-tech route.
- **You miss the "live" clues we discussed earlier.** When all you have is a tape of your lecture, you don't see that zealous flash in your teacher's eyes, the passionate arm-flailing, the stern set of the jaw, any and all of which should scream, "Pay attention. This will be on your test!"

Reading is fundamental

Reading improves reading. If you hate reading or consider yourself a slow reader, keep at it anyway. Read anything and everything. Read at night and on weekends. Read cereal boxes (even though the ingredients can often be as scary as a Stephen King novel) and newspapers and magazines and short stories and....well, you get the idea.

As you may have guessed by now, there's a volume in my ***How to Study Program*** on this topic, too. It's called ***Improve Your Reading*** (available in a brand-new fourth edition), and it provides a lot of detail on how you can get more out of your reading.

Let's look at how you can use your reading skills—and improve them—to get higher grades. Here are some suggestions that help people read more efficiently:

1. When a chapter in a textbook has questions at the end, read the questions first. Why? They will give you an idea of what the chapter is all about and they will be "clues" as to what you should look for in the text.
2. Some of the *words* in each chapter will help you concentrate on the important points and ignore the unimportant. Knowing when to speed up, slow down, ignore, or really concentrate will help you read both faster *and* more effectively.

   When you see words or phrases such as "likewise," "in addition," "moreover," or "furthermore," you should know nothing new is being introduced.

   When you see words and phrases such as "on the other hand," "nevertheless," "however," "rather," or "but," slow down—you're getting information that adds a new perspective or contradicts what you've just read.

   Lastly, watch out for payoff words and phrases such as, "in conclusion," "to summarize," "consequently," "thus"—especially if you only have time to hit the high points of a chapter.
3. Underline or highlight main points in the text. Pay special attention to words and phrases the author has highlighted by placing them in italics or in boldface.
4. Don't skip over the maps, charts, graphs, photos, or drawings. Much of this information may not be in the text. If you skip it, you're skipping vital information.
5. What's the big picture here? We can get bogged down in the footnotes and unfamiliar words and

lose touch with the purpose of the chapter. Keep these simple steps in mind:

- ✎ Rephrase headings as questions. This will support your purpose for reading.
- ✎ Examine all subheadings, illustrations, and graphics, as these will help you identify the significant matter within the text.
- ✎ Read the introductory paragraphs, summary, and end-of-chapter questions.
- ✎ Read the first sentence of every paragraph, generally where the main idea is found.
- ✎ Evaluate what you've gained from the process: Can you answer the questions at the chapter's end? Could you intelligently participate in a class discussion of the material?
- ✎ Write a brief summary of what you have learned from your skimming.

6. Shortly before class, look over the chapter again. Review what you and the author have decided are the most important points and mark topics you want the teacher to explain.

15 questions to help you

Beyond grasping the meaning of words and phrases, critical reading requires that you ask questions. Here are 15 questions that will help you effectively analyze and interpret most of what you read.

1. Is a clear message communicated throughout?
2. Are the relationships between the points direct and clear?
3. Is there a relationship between your experience and the author's?
4. Are the details factual?

5. Are the examples and evidence relevant?
6. Is there consistency of thought?
7. What is the author's bias or slant?
8. What is the author's motive?
9. What does the author want you to believe?
10. Does this jibe with your beliefs or experiences?
11. Is the author rational or subjective?
12. Is there a confusion between feelings and facts?
13. Are the main points logically ordered?
14. Are the arguments and conclusions consistent?
15. Are the explanations clear?

Obviously, this list of questions is not all-inclusive, but it will give you a jump start when critical reading is required. Remember, the essential ingredient to any effective analysis and interpretation is the questions you ask.

After class

The best time to study for your next class is right after the last one. Say you have Government 101 at 9:30 a.m. on Tuesday and Thursday. As soon as you can after your Tuesday class, review the day's notes, and complete the reading and homework for Thursday.

Why? Because the class is fresh in your mind. Your notes are crying out to be reviewed and corrected or added to, and you have a level of understanding that may not be there Wednesday night at 9 p.m.

Then, spend a little time on the same class and the same materials as close as possible to the next class. Let's say you can do that at 8:30 a.m. on Thursday. The *big* study time is ASAP after Tuesday's class; the little *quick-let's-review* time comes shortly *before* Thursday's class.

Now, let's refine these study habits for the next test.

CHAPTER 4

Study Smarter, Not Harder

> "You have to study a great deal to know a little."
>
> —Charles de Secondat, Baron de Montesquieu (1689-1755)

I'M GOING TO be so bold as to amend what the baron said: "You have to study a reasonable amount to know a great deal." Why change his centuries-old words? Because we know a lot about study techniques that he didn't and can concentrate on studying *smarter,* not harder.

Give your studies the time of day

As much as possible, create a routine time of day to study. Some students find it easier to set aside specific blocks of time during the day, each day, in which they plan on studying. In reality, the time of day you will do your work will be determined by a number of factors:

1. **Study when you're at your best.** What is your "peak performance period"—the time of day you do your best work? This varies from person to person—you may be dead to the world till noon but able to study well into the night. Or maybe you're up and alert at the crack of dawn but distracted and tired if you try to burn the midnight oil.
2. **Consider your sleep habits.** Habit is a powerful influence. If you always set your alarm for 7 a.m., you may find that you wake up then even when you forget to set it. If you are used to going to sleep around 11 p.m., you will undoubtedly get quite tired if you try to stay up studying until 2 a.m., and probably accomplish very little in the three extra hours.
3. **Study when you can.** Although you want to study when you're mentally most alert, external factors also play a role in deciding when you study. Being at your best is not always possible. Study whenever circumstances allow.
4. **Consider the complexity of the assignment when you allocate time.** The tasks themselves may have a great effect on your schedule. Study unit increments of an hour or two might work well for you most of the time. On the other hand, you may have no problem at all working on a long project in fits and starts, for 15 or 20 minutes at a time, without needing to retrace your steps each time you pick it up again.

Where should you study?

If you've never asked yourself this question—assuming that home is where the heart and the books are—take the time to discover both where you're most comfortable and most effective. Here are some possibilities:

At the library. There may be numerous choices, from the large reading room, to quieter, sometimes deserted specialty rooms, to your own study cubicle.

At home. Just remember that this is the place where distractions are most likely to occur. No one tends to telephone you at the library and little brothers (or your own kids) will not tend to find you easily in the "stacks."

At a friend's, neighbor's, or relative's house. This may not be an option for most of you, even on an occasional basis, but you may want to set up one or two alternative study sites.

In an empty classroom. Certainly an option at many colleges and perhaps some private high schools, it is a good idea mainly because so few students have ever thought of it!

At your job. Whether you're a student working part-time or fully employed and going to school part-time, you may be able to make arrangements to use an empty office, even during regular office hours, or perhaps after everyone has left (depending on how much your boss trusts you).

How to stay focused on your studies

Whatever location you choose as your "study base," how you set up your study area can affect your ability to stay focused and, if you aren't careful, seriously inhibit quality study time.

Sit down at your desk or study area right now and evaluate your own study environment:

1. Do you have one or two special places reserved just for studying? Or do you study wherever seems convenient or available at the time?
2. Is your study area a pleasant place? Would you offer it to a friend as a good place to study? Or do you dread it because it's so depressing?
3. How's the lighting? Is it too dim? Too bright? Is the whole desk well-lit? Or only portions of it?

4. Are all the materials you need handy?
5. What else do you do here? Eat? Sleep? Write letters? Read for pleasure? If you try to study at the same place you sit to listen to your music or chat on the phone, you may find yourself doing one when you think you're doing the other!
6. Is your study area in a high- or low-traffic area? How often are you interrupted by people passing through?
7. Can you close the door to the room to avoid disturbances and outside noise?
8. When do you spend the most time here? What time of day do you study? Is it when you are at your best, or do you inevitably study when you're tired and less productive?
9. Are your files, folders, and other class materials organized and near the work area? Do you have some filing system in place for them?

If you find yourself doodling and dawdling more than diagramming and deciphering, consider these solutions:

Create a work environment in which you're comfortable. The size, style, and placement of your desk, chair, and lighting may all affect whether or not you're distracted from the work at hand. Take the time to design the area that's perfect for you.

Turn up the lights. Experiment with the placement and intensity of lighting in your study area until you find what works for you, both in terms of comfort and as a means of staying awake and focused.

Set some rules. Let family, relatives, and especially friends know how important your studying is and that specific hours are inviolate.

Take the breaks you need. Don't follow some parent's or teacher's well-intentioned but bogus advice about how long you should study before taking a break. Take your breaks when *you* need to.

Fighting tiredness and boredom

You've chosen the best study spot and no one could fault you on its set up. So how come you're still using pencils to prop up your eyelids? Help is on the way:

Take a nap. What a concept! When you're too tired to study, take a short nap to revive yourself. The key is to maximize that nap's effect, and *that* means keeping it short—20 to 40 minutes.

Have a drink. A little caffeine won't harm you—a cup of coffee or tea, a glass of soda. Be careful not to mainline it—caffeine's "wake up" properties seem to reverse when you reach a certain level.

Turn down the heat. You needn't build an igloo, but too warm a room will leave you dreaming of sugarplums.

Shake a leg. Or anything else that peps you up. Go for a walk, high step around the kitchen, do jumping jacks—even mild physical exertion will give you an immediate lift.

Change your study schedule. Presuming you have some choice here, find a way to study when you are normally more awake and/or more efficient.

The King Tut Method

I use a method for studying called the Inverted Pyramid Theory. Simply picture a pyramid. The top is very wide, the bottom very narrow. This is symbolic of the way you should study for a test. Begin with all possible materials (all notes, book chapters, workbooks, audiotapes, and so forth) and briefly review everything to see what you need to spend time with and what you can put aside.

I also call this separating the wheat from the chaff. The wheat is the edible good stuff that's taken from the field and turned into Chocolate Sugar Munchies. The chaff stays behind. The chaff was important at one time but it no longer is needed. The same is true of some of your material you've gathered for this next test. Now try this:

1. Gather all the material you have been using for the course: books, workbooks, handouts, notes, homework, and previous tests and papers.
2. Compare the contents with the material you will be tested on and ask yourself: What exactly do I need to review for this test?
3. Select the material for review. Reducing the pile of books and papers will be a psychological aid—suddenly, it'll seem as if you have enough time and energy to study for the test.
4. Photocopy and complete the Pre-Test Organizer on pages 118 and 119. Consider carefully the "Material to be covered" section. Be specific. The more detailed you are, the better job you'll do in reviewing all the areas that you should know. This exercise will help you *quantify* what you need to do.
5. As you review the material and conclude that you know it for the test, put a bold check mark in the "Review" area. You are, to use my example, inverting the pyramid or shrinking the amount of material you need to study.
6. By the time the test is given, you should have reduced the "pyramid" to nothing. Go into the test and do well!

Flash yourself

You probably remember flash cards from elementary school. On one side was a picture, on the other a word. Or one side held a definition ("someone who studies bugs"), and the other the word being defined ("entomologist").

Using flash cards is a great way to test yourself. It also works for two people studying together or for a group. It works well for studying vocabulary, short answers, definitions, matching ("Boise" and "potato"), even true and false.

No person is an island

Don't face the Huguenots alone. Or even the periodic table of the elements. Share *your* knowledge while you benefit from the knowledge of a handful of other students in the same class. In other words, form a study group.

Try, if you can, to study with others who are at your level or slightly above. Notice I say *slightly* above. If you're a solid C and they're easy-A people, you won't connect. You'll want to review information they'll agree to skip. (The opposite will happen to *you* if you choose people too far below you.)

Study groups can be organized in a variety of ways. Each member could be assigned primary responsibility for a single class, including preparing detailed notes from lectures and discussion groups. If supplementary reading is recommended but not required, that person could be responsible for doing all such reading and preparing detailed summaries.

The extra work you will have to do in one class will be offset by the extra work others will be doing for you.

Alternatively, everybody can be responsible for his or her own notes, but the group could act as an ad hoc discussion group, refining your understanding of key points, working on problems, questioning each other, practicing for tests, and so forth.

Even if you find only one or two other students willing to work with you, such cooperation will be invaluable, especially in preparing for major exams.

I suggest four students minimum, probably six maximum. You want to ensure each person gets a chance to participate as much as he or she wants while maximizing the collective knowledge and wisdom of the group.

While group members needn't be best friends, they shouldn't be overtly hostile to one another, either. Seek diversity of experience, demand common dedication. Avoid a group in which you're the "star"—at least until you flicker out during the first exam.

Decide early on if you're forming a study group or a social group. If it's the latter, don't pretend it's the former. If it's the former, don't just invite your friends and informally sit around discussing your teachers for an hour a week.

Make meeting times and assignments formal and rigorous. Consider rigid rules of conduct. Ditch nonserious students early. You don't want anyone who is working as little as possible and taking advantage of *your* hard work.

However you choose to organize, clearly decide—early—the exact requirements and assignments of each student. Again, you never want the feeling to emerge that one or two of you are trying to "ride the coattails" of the others.

Learn from your mistakes

If you have access to old exams written by the same teacher, especially if they cover the same material you're going to be tested on, use them also for review.

Chances are the very same questions will *not* appear again. But the way the test is prepared, the kinds of questions, the emphasis on one kind of question over another (100 true/false, 50 multiple choice and one—count it—*one* essay), may well predict the design of your own test.

At the same time, see if you can find anyone who had this teacher for this class last year or last semester. Can they give you any advice, tips, hints, or warnings?

Once you've discovered the type of test facing you, you want to figure out what's going to be *on* it (and hence, what you need to study). Remember, it's rarely, if ever, "everything."

Take the time to eliminate from consideration, with the possible exception of a cursory review, material you are convinced is simply not important enough to be included on an upcoming test. This will automatically give you more time to concentrate on those areas you are sure *will* be included.

Then create a "To Study" list for each test. On it, list specific books to review, notes to recheck, and specific topics, principles, ideas, and concepts to go over. Check off each item as you study it. This method will minimize procrastination, logically organize your studying, and give you ongoing "jolts" of accomplishment as you complete each item.

All teachers are not equal (or fair or nice or...)

In an ideal world, all teachers would be filled with knowledge they eagerly and expertly shared with their students. Their lectures would be exciting and brief. Their tests would be fair and accurate measurements of what the students should have learned.

Before you tell me about pigs flying, let me say that, in spite of the criticism schools and teachers have been getting for years, there are a lot of teachers out there like that. If you don't think you've had one yet, your turn is coming.

In the meantime, though, let's consider Weird Al (or Weird Alice.) His personality may come out, unfortunately, when he writes and grades his tests. If you're lucky, you'll be forewarned by his former students so that you can be prepared as much as possible.

Watch for these danger signs. Even if he never seems to know when the next test will be, try to get that answer out of him. Believe me, you want to ask. It's better to discover today that it's a week from Thursday rather than finding out the Wednesday before.

If he says he doesn't know what the test will cover, keep asking him. Also ask what types of questions will be on the test (true/false, multiple choice, essays) and what percentage of the test will be devoted to each. By your questions, you are helping him shape the test in his mind, and giving him the information he needs to give back to you.

Once you've taken the test, check your corrected test paper carefully. If a right answer was marked wrong, let him know. If the question is too ambiguous and you think your answer could be right as well as the one *he* says is right, let him know. If you can explain your reasoning logically, most teachers will consider giving you credit.

It's just the SAT. Relax.

Well, you did it. You registered to take the SAT, the ACT, or some other supposedly life-altering test, and the Day of Reckoning is approaching.

While I'll share some specifics on taking *any* test in the next few chapters, for right now just remember that any hours-long national standardized test requires a lot of the same skills and the same planning as any unit quiz, chapter test, midterm, or final.

These standardized tests are intended to test your general knowledge of many areas, rather than grill you on the details from Chapter 14 of your chemistry book. They will seek to find out what you know about a lot of different subjects. Some of the answers will come from knowledge you gained years before. Others will come from your ability to work out the problems right there, using techniques and knowledge you gained this semester.

To prepare for any standardized test—the PSAT, SAT, ACT, GRE, GMAT, and so forth—I have one big suggestion: Determine, based on your past test-taking experiences and your comfort levels, what your weak areas are. Do you continually and completely mess up essay questions? Do analogies spin you out of control? Do you freeze at the sight of an isosceles triangle?

Seek out teachers, librarians, and school counselors who can guide you to samples of these kinds of questions. Ask your teachers and fellow students for advice on handling the areas you feel you are weak in, take the sample tests, and then work on evaluating how you did. Keep testing yourself and keep evaluating how you are doing.

Get advice from other students who say things like, "Analogies? Piece of cake!" Find out if they really can do them easily and get tips from them (and from what I say in the following chapters).

Also, a solid review of basic math and English will be valuable. If geometry is not your strong suit, find a book that contains lists of the fundamentals and spend time reviewing information that you will be expected to exercise on the SAT. Do the same with the other subject areas to be tested. If your library doesn't have such materials, get advice from teachers or from the counseling office.

You've probably been told for most of your life that your score on the SAT will determine whether you are a raving success eating in the finest restaurants or the busboy who cleans up afterwards. How vital is the SAT to the college admission process and, one presumes, to the rest of your life? Depending on whom you listen to, "very" or "not at all." According to Michele Hernandez, a former admissions officer at Dartmouth (quoted in the January 10, 1999 *New York Times Magazine*), "Deep down, admissions officers don't want SAT scores to count that much, but...they do." Yet in 1996, Harvard turned down 165 applicants sporting *perfect* SATs—800 on the verbal, 800 on the math. And more than 300 colleges no longer even require the SAT or ACT for admission.

Put me in, coach!

Should you take one of those test-preparation courses? Is it worth the money, the time, the effort, the bother?

The answer is a definite maybe. It depends on a handful of factors: First of all, ask others for recommendations. Listen closely to why they liked or disliked a particular course (their reasons may not match your reasons—tread carefully here). Ask particularly about each course's effectiveness and results.

Decide if you have the time and money to take a course. If you do, which kind do you want? There are coaching classes taught by people, but there are also book/cassette tape combos and computer programs. Ask your school counseling office for recommendations. The office may even have copies of some of the programs. If you don't have the money, ask about financial aid and other ways to reduce tuition.

Evaluate the professionalism of whatever course you're considering. How good are the materials? Do they look complete and professionally prepared, or do they consist of a sheaf of badly photocopied forms and a ratty binder? Can you attend a meeting free to get a feel for the procedures? Will they furnish you with the resumes of your instructors? Will those instructors be accessible outside of class?

Finally, are there any money-back guarantees? The best companies—in this or any field—stand behind their product, even if that means giving full refunds to dissatisfied customers.

There's method in their madness

The standardized-test coaching programs should deal with two areas. I'll call them method and content.

Method is the study of *how* to take a test, specifically how to take the PSAT, SAT, ACT, GRE, or whichever standardized test you happen to be preparing for. That portion of the course will cover much of the same material that you're reading in this book, especially the material we're going to look at in the next two chapters.

Content deals with practicing the sort of stuff that will be on the specific test you are taking: vocabulary words, math problems, essay questions, analogies, and so on.

The two areas overlap, of course. When you work math problems there are methods you utilize to get the answer, just as there is content.

Practicing for the SAT by answering questions that are similar in content to what you will later be tested on is a valuable exercise, but it's only half of the equation. The other half is the feedback you get from your coach (or teacher, counselor, or fellow students) on what you did, how you did, and why you did what you did. It won't do you any good to keep messing up on analogies, for example, if you can't stop and figure out how to do them right.

Important Note: As of this writing, many standardized tests are no longer offered "on paper," only on computer (CAT—for computer-adaptive testing format). Among the most important that fall into this category are the GMAT (Graduate Management Admissions Test), GRE (Graduate Record Exam), and TOEFL (Test of English as a Foreign Language), along with a number of specific licensing tests.

What does this mean to you? Tests available only in CAT format require a different strategy because of two important factors: You can't return to a previous answer, and you can't skip a question and return to it later. Make sure you know if you are taking a computer or written test and practice (and strategize) accordingly! Neither the SAT or PSAT are currently offered as CAT tests, but it surely won't be long until they are.

CHAPTER 5

Essay Tests: Write On!

"ACE" ANY TEST

ESSAY QUESTIONS. SOME students love them. Some hate them. Personally, I think *all* "objective" tests are harder than essay tests. Why? An objective test of any kind gives the teacher much more latitude, even the option of focusing *only* on the most obscure details (which, granted, only the truly sadistic would do). As a result, it's much more difficult to eliminate areas or topics when studying for such a test. It's also rare to be given a choice—answer 25 out of 50—whereas you may often be given, for example, five essay questions and have to choose only three. This greatly increases the odds that even sporadic studying will have at least given you some understanding about one or two of the questions, whereas you may be lost on a 100-question true-false test.

Less can go wrong on an essay test—there are only three or four questions to read, not 100 potential *mis*reads. It's also easier to budget time among three or four essay questions than among 150 multiple-choice ones.

Whether you love or hate essays, there are some important pointers to ensure that you at least score better on them.

Of course you know this, but...

Really advanced schools with big budgets provide typewriters or computers for their students so they can write essays in the classroom. But we can't all have 90210 as our ZIP code. The rest of you will have to work with a pen.

First of all, make sure it's a good pen. One that you're comfortable with. If you hate ballpoints and swear by felt-tipped pens, then go for it. Actually, go for *them*. Only someone who wants a really bad grade shows up with one pen. Naturally, it will run out, begin to leak, break, or all of the above. If you have two (or, for the truly superstitious, three or more) then, of course, the first pen will be working like that annoying drum-beating rabbit when your grandchildren are taking the SAT on Mars.

Think before you ink

Approach essay questions the same way you would a paper. While you can't check your textbook or go to the library to do research, the facts, ideas, and formulas, you need are in your own cerebral library—your mind.

Don't ever, *ever* begin writing the answer to an essay question without a little "homework" first. I don't care if you're the school's prize-winning journalist.

First, really look at the question. Are you sure you know what it's asking? What are the verbs? Don't "describe" when it calls for you to "compare and contrast."

Don't "explain" when it tells you to "argue." Underline the verbs. (See page 79 for a list of the most-used verbs in essay tests and what each is instructing you to do.) And please don't, intentionally or otherwise, misread the question in such a way that you answer the question you'd like rather than the one you've actually been given.

Then sit back a minute and think about what you are going to say. Or spend less than a minute, depending on how much time you have, but *don't* just start writing.

Here's a step-by-step way to answer essay questions:

Step one: On a blank sheet of paper, write down all the facts, ideas, concepts, and details you feel should be included in your answer. (If you don't have extra paper, the back of your blue book or the test itself will work just as well.)

Step two: Organize them in the order in which they should appear. You don't have to rewrite your notes into a detailed outline—why not just number each note according to where you want to place it?

Step three: Compose your first paragraph. It should summarize and introduce the key points you will make in your essay. *This is where superior essay answers are made or unmade.*

Step four: Write your essay, with your penmanship as legible as possible. Most teachers I've known do *not* go out of their way to decipher chicken scratch masquerading as an essay and do *not* award high grades to it either.

Step five: Reread your essay and, if necessary, add points left out, correct spelling, grammar, and so on.

If there is a particular fact you know is important and should be included but you just don't remember it, take a guess. Otherwise, just leave it out and do the best you can.

Remember: Few teachers will be impressed by length. A well-organized, well-constructed, and specific answer will always get you a better grade than randomly writing down everything you know in the faint hope that you will actually hit something.

Start with a brief, to-the-point first paragraph that doesn't meander or "pad." ("What were the similarities between Dante's Beatrice and Joyce's Molly Bloom? To truly answer this question, we must first embark upon a study of Italian and Irish literature, politics, and culture at the time..." Have we wasted enough of our precious time trying to cover up our lack of knowledge here?) End your essay with a clearly written and organized paragraph that offers more than just a summation of what you've already written.

Worry less about the specific words and more about the information. Organize your answer to a fault and write to be understood, not to impress. Better to use shorter sentences, paragraphs, and words—and be clear and concise—than to let the teacher fall into a clausal nightmare from which he may never emerge (and neither will your A!).

If you don't have the faintest clue what the question means, ask. If you still don't have any idea of the answer—and I mean *zilch*—leave it blank. Writing down everything you think you know about the supposed subject in the hopes that one or two things will actually have something to do with the question is, in my mind, a waste of everyone's time. Better to allocate the time you would waste to other parts of the test and do a better job on those.

The best-organized beats the best-written

Although I think numbering your notes is as good an organizational tool as jotting down a complete outline, there is certainly nothing wrong with fashioning a quick outline. Not one with Roman numerals—this outline will consist of a simple list of abbreviated words, scribbled on a piece of scrap paper or in the margin of your test booklet.

The purpose of this outline is the same as that of those fancy ones: to make sure you include everything you need and want to say—in order.

It's important to write well. But excellent writing, even pages and pages of it, will not get you an excellent grade unless you write quality answers—hard-hitting, incisive, and direct.

Think of the introduction and the conclusion as the bread in a sandwich, with the information in between as the hamburger, lettuce, tomato, and pickle. Everything is necessary for it all to hang together, but the main attraction is going to be what's between the slices.

Give me some space, man

Plan ahead. Write your essay on every other line and on one side of the paper or page only. This will give you room to add or correct anything without having to write it so small that it is illegible and, therefore, doesn't earn you any credit.

Proof it!

Budget your time so that you can go back over your essay, slowly, and correct any mistakes or make any additions. Check your spelling, punctuation, grammar, and syntax. (If you don't know what syntax is, find out. You'll need to know for the SAT.) It would be a shame for you to write a beautiful, thorough essay and lose points because of careless errors.

When you're done, you're done...almost

Resist the temptation to leave the room or turn in your paper before you absolutely have to. Take the time at the end of the test to review not only your essay answers, but your other answers as well. Make sure all words and numbers are readable. Make sure you have matched the right question and the right answer. Even make sure you didn't miss a whole section by turning over a page too quickly or not noticing that a page was missing.

If you're out of time, are you out of luck?

While you should have carefully allocated sufficient time to complete each essay before you started working on the first, things happen. You may find yourself with two minutes left and one full essay to go. What do you do? As quickly as possible, write down every piece of information you think should be included in your answer, and number each point in the order in which you would have written it. If you then have time to reorganize your notes into a better-organized outline, do so. Many teachers will give you at least partial credit if your outline contains all the information the answer was supposed to. It will at least show you knew a lot about the subject and were capable of outlining a reasonable response.

One of the reasons you may have left yourself with insufficient time to answer one or more questions is you knew too darned much about the previous question(s), and you wanted to make sure the teacher *knew* you knew, so you wrote...and wrote...and wrote...until you ran out of time.

Be careful—some teachers throw in a relatively general question that, if you wanted to, you could write about until next Wednesday. In that case, they aren't testing your knowledge of the whole subject as much as your ability to *edit* yourself, to organize and summarize the *important* points.

Common instructional verbs on essay tests

Compare. Examine two or more objects, ideas, people, etc., and note similarities and differences.

Contrast. Compare to highlight differences. Similar to *differentiate, distinguish.*

Criticize. Judge and discuss merits and faults. Similar to *critique.*

Define. Explain the nature or essential qualities.

Describe. Convey the appearance, nature, attributes, etc.

Discuss. Consider or examine by argument, comment, etc.; debate; explore solutions.

Enumerate. List various events, things, descriptions, ideas, etc.

Evaluate. Appraise the worth of an idea, comment, etc., and justify your conclusion.

Explain. Make the meaning of something clear, plain, intelligible, and/or understandable.

Illustrate. Use specific examples or analogies to explain.

Interpret. Give the meaning of something by paraphrase, by translation, or by an explanation based on personal opinion.

Justify. Defend a statement or conclusion. Similar to *support.*

Narrate. Recount the occurrence of something, usually by giving details of events in the order in which they occurred. Similar to *describe,* but only applicable to something that happens in time.

Outline. Do a general sketch, account, or report, indicating only the main features of a book, subject, or project.

Prove. Establish the truth or genuineness by evidence or argument. Similar to *show, explain why, demonstrate.* (In math, verify validity by mathematical demonstration.)

Relate. Give an account of events and/or circumstances, usually to establish associations, connections, or relationships.

Review. Survey a topic, occurrence, or idea, generally but critically. Similar to *describe, discuss, illustrate, outline, summarize, trace.* Some test makers may use these words virtually interchangeably, although one can find subtle differences in each.

State. Present the facts concisely. May be used interchangeably with *name, list, indicate, identify, enumerate, cite.*

Summarize. State in concise form, omitting examples and details.

Trace. Follow the course or history of an occurrence, idea, etc.

CHAPTER 6

Objective Tests: Discriminate and Eliminate

SOME PEOPLE PREFER objective tests to essays. After all, in multiple-choice questions, the answer is staring you in the face (and secretly sticking out its tongue at you, if you don't recognize it). You just have to be able to figure out which one it is.

In this chapter, we're going to look at the different types of objective questions, along with some of the methods to use to answer each type, based primarily on "the process of elimination."

If you learn nothing else from this chapter, learn this: The process of elimination has saved many a person from failure. It may just save you.

Place sprocket A into dovetail Y

A very key point of preparation for *any* kind of test: Read and understand the directions. Otherwise, you could seemingly do everything *right,* but not follow your teacher's explicit directions, in which case everything's *wrong.*

If you're supposed to check off every correct answer to each question in a multiple-choice test—and you're assuming only *one* answer to each question is correct—you're going to miss a lot of answers!

If you're to pick one essay question out of three, or two out of five, that's a lot different than trying to answer every one. You won't be able to do it. Even if you do, the teacher will probably only grade the first two. Because you needed to allocate enough time to do the other three, it's highly doubtful your first two answers will be so detailed and so perfect that they will be able to stand alone.

In the case of a standardized test, such as the PSAT, SAT, ACT, or GRE, read the instructions on a previous test before you go to the test site. (There are numerous books that include "actual tests," and practice tests can be downloaded from many Web sites as well.) Then just skim the instructions in your booklet or on the computer to make sure nothing has changed. It will save you minutes, time that is precious indeed during any such test.

Are the questions or sections weighted? Some tests may have two, three, or more sections, some of which count for very little—10 or 20 percent of your final score—while one, usually a major essay, may be more heavily weighted—50 percent or more of your grade. Let this influence the amount of energy you devote to each section.

I know students who, before they write a single answer, look through the entire test and break it down into time segments—allocating 20 minutes for section one, 40 for section two, and so forth. Even on multiple-choice tests, they count the total number of questions, divide by the time allotted, and set "goals" on what time they should reach question 10, question 25, and so on.

If there are pertinent facts or formulas you're afraid you'll forget, I think it's a good idea to write them down somewhere in your test booklet before you do anything else. It won't take much time and it could save some serious memory jogs later.

When a guess isn't just a guess

Will you be penalized for guessing? The teacher may inform you that you will earn two points for every correct answer, but *lose* one point for every incorrect one. This will certainly affect whether you guess or skip the question—or, at the very least, how many potential answers you feel you need to eliminate before the odds of guessing are in your favor. (As far as the SAT is concerned, there really isn't a penalty for guessing, so don't leave an answer blank!)

If there's no penalty for wrong answers, you should *never* leave an answer blank. But you should also do everything you can to increase your odds of getting it right. If every multiple-choice question gives you four possible answers, you have a 25-percent chance of being right (and, of course, a 75-percent chance of being wrong) each time you have to guess.

But if you can eliminate a single answer—one you are reasonably certain cannot be right—your chances of being correct increase to 33 percent.

And, of course, if you can get down to a choice between two answers, it's just like flipping a coin: 50-50. In the long run, you will guess as many right as wrong.

Even if there is a penalty for guessing, I would probably pick one answer if I had managed to increase my chances of getting the right one to 50-50.

Presuming that you've managed to eliminate one or more answers but are still unsure of the correct answer and have no particular way to eliminate further, here are some real insider tips to make your "guess" more educated:

- If two answers sound alike, choose neither.
- The most "obvious" answer to a difficult question is probably wrong, but an answer that is close to it is probably right.
- If the answers that are left to a mathematical question cover a broad range, choose the number in the middle.
- If two quantities are very close, choose one of them.
- If two numbers differ only by a decimal point (and the others aren't close), choose one of them.
- If two answers to a mathematical problem *look* alike—either formulas or shapes—choose one of them.

Remember: This is not the way to ace a test—these are just some tried-and-true ways to increase your guessing power when *you have absolutely nothing else to go on and nothing left to do.*

Eliminate the sort-of obvious

Suppose the question was as follows: "The first U.S. President to appoint a woman to the Cabinet was (A) Franklin D. Roosevelt, (B) Herbert Hoover, (C) Abraham Lincoln, or (D) Jimmy Carter."

Most likely, you can get the answer down to two choices pretty quickly. You're absolutely correct to eliminate, right away, Abraham Lincoln. It wasn't that he was a bad guy; you just have to remember that women didn't even have the right to vote at that time, and laws and customs kept women from doing most of what they are doing today.

You may be fuzzy on who was in Jimmy Carter's Cabinet (he may have been fuzzy, too), but even if you are too young to remember Carter, you're guessing that he was recent enough not to be the first president to appoint women in that role.

If you have any knowledge of history, and I hope you do, you know that the two remaining choices were, at least, presidents during the 20th century...in other words, after women were granted the right to vote.

You may not be able to get past this choice. But, even if you can't, and you blindly select one or the other, your chance of selecting the correct answer is one out of two. Even if your teacher deducts points, I would go ahead and put down (A) or (B).

Those of you who know a little more about history are going to remember that Roosevelt was loved or hated for his dramatic changes in government, while Hoover was the poster boy for The Status Quo Society. If that difference in their styles and actions comes to mind, then you'd be 100 percent correct to choose FDR.

Check it out, check it out!

Use this process of elimination for all types of objective questions. Depending on whether you can eliminate any of the answers and whether you feel you can "afford" to lose the points will help you decide how to answer the question.

If there is time during a test for you to come back to questions and look at them one more time, go ahead and put a line through the answers you know can't be correct. That will simply save you time. You will ignore the answers that are struck out and concentrate on the ones that remain.

What if you eliminate four out of five answers and are convinced the one that's left—your "right" answer—is definitely wrong? Eliminate *it* and start your process of elimination all over again with the other four.

Should you go back, recheck your work, and change a guess? How valid was that first guess? It was probably pretty darn good (presuming you had some basis for guessing in the first place). So good that you should *only* change it *if*:

- ✎ It really was just a wild guess and, upon further thought, you conclude your guess answer really should be eliminated (in which case your next guess is, at least, not quite so wild).
- ✎ You remembered something that changed the odds of your guess completely (or the answer to a later question helped you figure out the answer to this one!).
- ✎ You miscalculated on a math problem.
- ✎ You misread the question (didn't notice a "not," "always," or another important qualifier).

Get visual

Throughout a test, don't miss an opportunity to draw a picture for yourself if this will help you understand the question and figure out the right answer. If the question deals with any sort of cause-and-effect that has several steps in it, literally draw or write down those steps very quickly, using abbreviated words or symbols. This may help you see missing pieces, help you understand relationships between parts, and, thus, help you select the right answer.

Multiple-choice test tips

1. Be careful you don't read too much into questions. Don't try to second-guess the test-preparer, get too elaborate, and ruin the answer.
2. Underline the key words.
3. If two choices are very similar, the answer is probably not either one of them.

4. If two choices are opposite, one of them is probably correct.
5. Don't go against your first impulse unless you are *sure* you were wrong. (Sometimes you're so smart you scare yourself.)
6. Check for negatives and other words that are there to throw you off. ("Which of the following is *not*....")
7. The answer is usually wrong if it contains "all," "always," "never," or "none." I repeat, usually.
8. The answer has a great chance of being right if it has "sometimes," "probably," or "some."
9. When you don't know the right answer, look for the wrong ones.
10. Don't eliminate an answer unless you actually know what every word means.
11. Read every answer. A sneaky test-maker will place a decoy answer that's *almost* right (or *seems* logically right) first, tempting you to pick it before you've even considered the other choices.
12. If it's a standardized test, consider transferring all the answers from one section to the answer sheet at the same time. This can save time.
13. If you're supposed to read a long passage and answer questions about it, read the questions *first*. That will tell you what you're looking for and *affect the way you read the passage*. (When you first read the question, before you look at the answers, decide what you think the answer is. If your answer is one of the choices, bingo!)
14. The longest and/or most complicated answer to a question is often correct—the test maker has been forced to add qualifying clauses or phrases to make that answer complete.

15. Be suspicious of choices that seem obvious to a 2-year-old. Why would the teacher give you such a gimme? Maybe she's not, that trickster!
16. Don't give up on a question that, after one reading, seems hopelessly confusing or hard. Looking at it from another angle, restating it in your own words, or drawing a picture may help you realize it's not as hard as you thought.

Analogies: Study/succeed as eat/live

To help you figure out the right answer in an analogy, write it out or at least *think* it out. Suppose the question was:

TIRED: SLEEP

(A) athletic: swim

(B) happy: wedding

(C) hungry: eat

(D) cold: blanket

What's the relationship between "tired" and "sleep"? First of all, what parts of speech are "tired" and "sleep" in this example? Adjective: verb. The correct answer is going to have the same relationship. Two of the answers, (B) and (D), are adjective: noun. So you've eliminated two of the four already.

What is the relationship between "tired" and "sleep"? "Sleep" is something you do when you are "tired." Which now seems correct? Athletic or hungry? If you substitute "hungry" and "eat" in the above sentence, doesn't it sound correct? But if you put "athletic" and "swim" in the same places, does it make sense? Certainly people who are athletic swim, but many athletes do not—and many people who aren't athletes may swim.

Some samples for you to taste

Many of these basic principles apply to the other types of questions you'll find on an objective test. Matching one item with another, completing sentences, doing math problems, choosing the correct vocabulary word—they all rely on:

1. (a) Your prior knowledge gained from studying for this particular course.
   (b) All the reading, studying, and listening you've been doing for years.
2. Your common sense.
3. Your ability to eliminate as many as possible of the potential answers.
4. Paying close attention to and following directions.

Let's run through an example of another type of question, this one involving antonyms (even though they're gone, thankfully, from the SAT):

IMPORTANT:
(A) significant
(B) trivial
(C) reciprocal
(D) consequential

The test writer has thrown in (A) to see if you'll flub up and choose a synonym. Not exactly dirty pool, but a technique to watch for. Choice (C) is a kind of off-center joke. Some people think that, because it is so unusual, it must be right. Answer (D) is a variation on (A), so the correct answer must be (B).

Comprehension questions

This is the portion of the test where you find a short essay, followed by several questions. You are supposed to find the answers to those questions in the essay. Unlike the multiple-choice questions, where the answer is actually right in front of you, the answers to the essay questions may well be hidden in one fashion or another.

Not since 3rd grade have you had an essay question that asks, "How old was John F. Kennedy when he married Jacqueline Bouvier?" and, lo and behold, back in the essay it clearly says, "John F. Kennedy was 36 years old when he married Jacqueline Bouvier." Unfortunately for you, those questions went out with notes that said, "Do you love me? Yes or No!" and recess.

You're lucky if you get questions like, "How old was John F. Kennedy when he was elected president?" and the essay says, "John F. Kennedy took office 21 years after graduating *cum laude* from Harvard in 1940."

Buried somewhere else in the essay will be something like, "Kennedy was born in 1917, the second of nine children born to Joseph and Rose Kennedy." Since you should know that Kennedy took office in 1961, you can figure out that he was 43 years old when he was elected in 1960. The rest is history.

Don't confuse me with facts

Here's the method I recommend for answering comprehension questions:

1. Read the questions first. Consider them clues in a puzzle. You'll be alerted to what the essay is about so you don't start cold.
2. Slowly read the essay, keeping in mind the questions you've just read. Don't underline too much, but do underline conjunctions that change the direction of the sentence: "however," "although," "nevertheless," "yet," and so forth.

Because of this shift, there is a good chance that this sentence will figure in one of the questions.

3. Read the questions again. Then go back and forth, finding out the answer to the first one, the second one, and so forth. Don't skip around unless the first question is an absolute stumper. If you jump around too much, you'll get confused again and you won't answer any of the questions very completely or even correctly.

You're failing this test: True or false?

I think true-false tests are generally more insidious than multiple-choice tests, because the latter at least offers the correct answer, which you may pick out without knowing it's correct. That's the bad news.

The good news is that it's hard to beat 50-50 odds!

What can you do to increase your scores on true-false tests? Be more inclined to guess if you have to. After all, I encouraged you to guess on a multiple-choice test if you could eliminate enough wrong answers to get down to two, one of which is correct. Well, you're already there! So, unless you are being penalized for guessing, guess away! Even if you are being penalized, you may want to take a shot if you have the faintest clue of the correct answer.

What tricks do test makers incorporate in true-false tests? Here are some to watch out for:

Two parts (statements) that *are* true (or at least *may* be true), linked in such a way that the *whole* statement becomes false. Example: "Because many birds can fly, they use stones to grind their food." Many birds *do* fly, and birds *do* swallow stones to grind their food. But a *causal relationship* (the word "because") between the two clauses makes the *whole* statement false. The longer and/or more complicated a statement in a true-false test, the less likely it's true because every clause of it must be true (and there are so many chances for a single part of it to be false).

Few broad, general statements are true *without exception.* So always be on your guard when you see the words "all," "always," "no," "never," or other absolutes. As long as you can think of a *single* example that proves such a statement false, then it's false. But be wary: There are statements with such absolutes that *are* true; they are just rare. "All U.S. presidents have been men" is, unfortunately, all too true.

Matching

Match the following countries with their capitals:

Berlin	Chile
Athens	China
Santiago	Greece
Beijing	Germany

Match the obvious ones first. Let's say you know Berlin and Beijing are the capitals of Germany and China, respectively. Look at the two remaining choices. Here is where common sense and good general knowledge will come in handy.

Because you probably get a lot of your world news from the radio and TV, you may well have heard the combos more than you've seen them. Go with the ones that "sound right." (In this case, Athens, Greece and Santiago, Chile.)

Sentence completions

Like many of the other kinds of problems, sentence completions can often be figured out by putting the question into context or into perspective. Here's an example:

The clerk at the clothing boutique asked the woman, "What's your ___?"

(A) age
(B) size
(C) color
(D) religion

Of course a sales clerk could ask her customers about their ages, colors, and religions, but in a clothing boutique, asking a customer's size makes the most sense.

Multiple-choice math

Process of elimination is important in finding the answers. There are some numbers to consider, also. For example, look at the problem below and see if you can figure out the answer without actually doing the math:

334 x 412 =
(A) 54,559
(B) 137,608
(C) 22,528
(D) 229,766

By performing one simple task, you can eliminate two of the possible answers. Multiply the last digits in each number (2 x 4). The answer must end in 8. So (A) and (D) have been eliminated...that fast!

Now, eyeball (B) and (C). Can you find the right answer quickly? Here you are doing educated guessing, known in math circles as "guesstimating." Look: 334 x 100 is 33,400, so (C) has to be wrong. You are left with (B).

Should you do the actual math to double-check your answer? I wouldn't. You are certain that (A) and (D) are wrong. Absolutely. You know that (C) is much too low. Mark (B) as the answer and move on.

Here are other ways to better your score on math tests:

- ✎ Try to figure out what is being asked, what principles are involved, what information is important, and what's not. Don't let extraneous data throw you off track. Make sure you know the *kind* of answer you're seeking: Is it a speed, weight, angle, exponent, square root?
- ✎ Whenever you can, "translate" formulas and numbers into words. Estimate the answer before you even begin the actual calculation.
- ✎ Even if you're not particularly visual, pictures can often help. Try translating a particularly vexing math problem into a drawing or diagram.
- ✎ Play around. There are often different paths to the same solution, or even equally valid solutions.
- ✎ When you are checking your calculations, try working *backwards*. I've found it an easier way to catch simple arithmetical errors.
- ✎ Try to write down all of your calculations—neatly. You'll be less likely to make a mistake if you take your time, and if you *do* make a mistake, it will be a lot easier to spot.
- ✎ Show every step and formula, even if you would normally skip a few. If you knew all of the principles and formulas but miscalculated near the very beginning of your analysis, you are not going to arrive at the correct answer. *But* many enlightened math teachers will take very little off if they can clearly see you knew your stuff and managed to do everything right, with the sole exception of hitting the right button on your calculator.

The importance of words

No matter how much you study principles and examples, you will be lost if the words used in the test are simply not in *your* vocabulary. I could make the point, of course, that without a sufficient vocabulary, you won't be able to keep up with the principles anyway. Like reading itself, building a workable vocabulary is absolutely essential to doing well on any kind of test, since you are more likely to understand the directions, the questions, and the possible answers.

Build your vocabulary as much as you can. Read good books. Listen to people who have large vocabularies. Write down words you don't know and become familiar with them. The more words you know, the better you can play the process of elimination game and the better score you'll get. I highly recommend *Better Vocabulary in 30 Minutes a Day* by Edie Schwager (Career Press, 1996), for those of you who are word-challenged.

All of the above, none of the above

Some teachers have fallen in love with "all of the above" and "none of the above." You can't take one of their tests without those phrases appearing in every other question. "All of the above" is often the right answer if it is an option. *Hope* that you see it as a potential answer to *every* question because *it gives you a much better chance to do better on the test* than your mastery of the material (or lack thereof) might normally warrant. Why? Because you don't have to be really sure that "all of the above" is correct to choose it. All you have to be is *pretty* sure that *two* answers are correct (and equally sure the others are not *necessarily* wrong). As long as there is—you feel—more than one correct answer, then "all of the above" must be the right choice!

Likewise, you don't have to be convinced that "none of the above" is the right answer, just *reasonably* sure that none of the other answers are absolutely correct.

Here's a sample analysis to show you why you should love teachers infatuated with "all" and "none":

> Which of the following authors won the Nobel Peace Prize for Literature in the 1990s?
>
> (A) Gunter Grass
> (B) Toni Morrison
> (C) Seamus Heaney
> (D) All of the above
> (E) None of the above

Do you know for a fact that one of them *didn't* win? If so, you *eliminate* (D). Do you know whether *any* of them won? If so, eliminate (E). Do you know if *two* of them won? Let's say you know that Toni Morrison was a winner in 1993 and that Gunter Grass won in 1999, but you've never even heard of Seamus Heaney. *Doesn't matter*—once you know *two* won, (D) is the *only* possible answer.

A word about "easy" tests

Some people think "open-book" tests are the easiest of all. They pray for them...at least until they see their first one.

These are the toughest tests of all, if only because even normally "nice" teachers feel no compunction whatsoever about making such tests as tough as a Marine drill instructor. *Heck, you can use your book!* That's like having a legal crib sheet, right? Worse yet, many open-book tests are also take-home tests, meaning you can use your notes (and any other books or tools you can think of).

Because you have to anticipate that there will be no easy questions, no matter how well you know that material, you need to do some preparation before you deal with this type of test.

- Mark important pages by turning down corners, using paper clips, or any other method that will help you quickly flip to important charts, tables, summaries, or illustrations.
- Write an index of the pages you've turned down so you know where to turn immediately for a specific chart, graph, table, and so forth.
- Summarize all important facts and formulas on a separate sheet.
- If you are also allowed to bring your notes or it's a take-home test, write a brief index to your notes (general topics only) so you know where to find pertinent information.

Answer the questions you don't need the book for first, including those of which you're fairly sure and know where to check the answers in your book. Star the latter ones.

Then use the book. Check starred answers first and erase the stars once you have completed them. Then work on those questions on which you must rely fully on the book.

While a take-home test is, by definition, an open-book test, it is the hardest of all. An open-book test in class simply can't last longer than the time allotted for the class. A take-home exam may give you a night or two, in some cases a week or longer, to complete.

Why are they so hard? You're *given* so much time because teachers expect that it will take you *longer* than the time available in class to finish. You may have to go well beyond your text(s) and notes even to get a handle on some of the questions, leading to some long nights at the library.

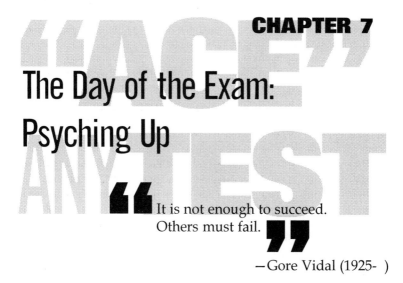

CHAPTER 7

The Day of the Exam: Psyching Up

> It is not enough to succeed.
> Others must fail. 
>
> —Gore Vidal (1925-)

ELL, HERE YOU are. No longer are you thinking of the exam as being next month or next week or even tomorrow. You're sitting in the very room in the very chair and someone is heading your way with a test paper.

The lifesaving bunch of stuff

Now that you're safely there, on time, what did you bring with you?

I used to make up what I called the Test Kit. Into my backpack went some pens or pencils (depending on what I needed for the test)—two or three of each; the book and workbooks associated with the test; my notes; a calculator, if allowed; a candy bar or other treat that would give me energy; photo ID; and an entry card, if required.

By collecting all this mess in one place, I wouldn't be very likely to forget it. Also, if I did something dreadful like oversleep, I only had to grab the one thing that I had packed the night before and dash out the door.

You have enough to worry about on the morning of a big test. Don't spend frantic minutes looking for something that you could have placed inside a backpack, briefcase or large purse the night before. Be kind to yourself.

Unless you are already in an assigned seat, try to sit near the front so you will get the exam first and have some precious seconds at the end while the other papers are being passed to the front. It also places you near the teacher or proctor for easier access for questions.

Avoid sitting near someone who has a lot of noisy jewelry, who is cracking or popping gum, or who is too friendly with the others in the immediate area. Be a hermit, in other words. Choose a quiet area.

Wear loose, comfortable clothes, the kind that you love, your favorite shirt or sweater or slacks. If you're left-handed, look for a left-handed desk. Check out the room for sunlight (too much or too little), lighting, and temperature.

Begin at the beginning. Then move through to the end. No, I'm not talking about taking the exam, I'm talking about looking through the booklet or taking a glance at all the questions. If you have permission to go all the way through it, do that before you ever start. Just give yourself an overview of what lies ahead. That way you can spot the easier sections (and do them first) and get an idea of the point values assigned to each section.

You can also make sure your test is complete. Wouldn't it feel terrible to flash through the test, check your answers with minutes to spare, and *then* discover you missed that last essay question...the one that counts for 50 percent of your grade?

The art of war

There are three ways to attack a multiple-choice test:

1. Start at the first question and keep going until you reach the end, never leaving a question until you have either answered it fully or made an educated guess.
2. Answer the *easy* questions first—the ones you know the answers to without any thinking at all or those requiring the simplest calculations—then go back and do the harder ones.
3. Answer the *hardest* questions first, then go back and do the easy ones.

None of these three options is inherently right or wrong. Each may work for different individuals. (I'm assuming that these three approaches are all in the context of the test format. Weighted sections may well affect your strategy.)

The first approach is, in one sense, the quickest, in that no time is wasted reading through the whole test trying to pick out either the easiest or hardest questions. Presuming that you do not permit yourself to get stumped by a single question so you spend an inordinate amount of time on it, it is probably the method most of you usually employ.

The second approach ensures that you will maximize your right answers—you're putting off those that you find particularly vexing.

Many experts recommend this method because they maintain that answering so many questions one after another gives you immediate confidence to tackle the questions you're not sure about. If you find that you agree, then by all means use this strategy. However, you may consider just *noting* the easy ones as you proofread the test. This takes less time and, to me, delivers the same "confidence boost."

The last approach is actually the one I used. In fact, I made it a point to do the very hardest questions first, then work my way "down" the difficulty ladder. (This means I often worked *backwards,* because many test makers and teachers make their tests progressively more difficult.)

It may sound like a strange strategy to you, so let me explain the psychology.

First of all, I figured if time pressure starts getting to me toward the end of the test, I would rather be in a position to answer the easiest questions—and lots of them—in the limited time left than ones I really had to think about.

That's the major benefit of the third approach: When I was most "up," most awake, most alert, I tackled the questions that required the most analysis, thinking, and interpretation. When I was most tired—near the end—I was answering the questions that are virtually "gimmes."

At the same time, I was also giving myself a *real* shot of confidence. As soon as I finished the first hard question, I already felt better. When I finished all of the hard ones, everything was downhill.

I would always, however, try to ensure adequate time to at least put down an answer for every question. Better to get one question wrong and complete three other answers than to get one right and leave three blank.

Ask questions immediately if you don't understand something. The proctor may not be able to say anything (or may not know anything to say), but it's worth a try.

If you get part of a question answered and you need to return to finish it, work out a little code for yourself. Put a symbol in the margin beside the problem that means "You're partly done here—come back to this one after you've done all the ones you can do."

Guess and guess again?

If you do guess at any of the objective questions and you are getting your test paper returned to you, place a little dot or other symbol beside them. That way you will know how successful your guessing was. For example, suppose you guessed at 30 questions and got 22 of them right. That tells me your guesses are, for the most part, *educated* guesses, not wild stabs in the dark, and that you earned enough points to make it worthwhile, *even if you got penalized for missing eight others*. However, if you only got six right, review my comments on educated guessing. Something's not working right for you.

When you think you have finished with a whole section, double-check to see if that's true. Look on the answer sheet or in the blue book to make sure all the questions have been answered.

It's a long race—pace yourself

If you have 100 multiple-choice questions and you have 50 minutes allotted for that section, you don't have to be MIT material to figure that you should spend a maximum of 30 seconds on each answer. Check your progress two or three times during the 50 minutes.

You say oral and I say aural

Listen up. When the teacher (or tape recorder) gives you a question, jot down the key words so that you can refer to them when you think up your answer.

Do the same thing if you are being given a dictation where you are expected to listen, and then write down what you heard. Key words—the nouns and verbs—will help you "capture" the rest of the sentence.

If you don't understand the question (whether it's in a foreign language you're studying or in English), ask to have it repeated. Ask again if you still don't understand. Listen intently to everything.

For computer-scored tests

If you are required to color in a little rectangle to show which answer is correct so that a machine can score the results, mark the answer sheet very carefully. Stray pencil marks can be picked up by the computer, causing the wrong answer to be recorded. If you carefully filled in one box, only to change your mind later, completely, *completely* erase the first answer. If the computer picks up both markings, guess what happens? You don't get the point, even if one of the boxes is correct.

You deserve a break today

Take the breaks that are offered. You'll benefit in the long run by going to the bathroom, getting a drink of water, eating a candy bar, or all of the above, rather than sitting there working through another algebraic equation. Just as you needed the good sleep you got during the week, you'll need to be energized by the breaks.

Now flex, one, two...

You can perform some unobtrusive exercises at your desk that will make you feel refreshed. Try them right now. First, tense up your feet—squeeze them hard, then relax them, then squeeze them. Then do the same with the muscles in your calves, shoulders, hips, and abdomen. It's a pretty simple exercise, but I find it energizes me when I am unable to get up and move around the room. Even moving the facial muscles helps. Do them looking down at your paper; otherwise your teacher will think you are having a coronary or making faces at her.

If there is time at the end of the test, review. Go back and check over answers to essay questions that may not be as complete as you'd like them to be, or look again at the unanswered questions in any other section.

If you have even more time, look at the "guess" questions you've marked. Does anything suddenly make sense, making you change your mind? Remember what I said about going with your first choice, but if you suddenly remember that the Catskills are in New York and not in North Dakota, change the answer!

CHAPTER 8

Post-test: Survival and Review

> "Winning isn't everything, but wanting to win is."
>
> —Vince Lombardi (1913-1970)

> "Winning is everything."
>
> —your mother

No, it's not. But you and I can understand what Mom's talking about, right? It's nice to win, whether it's a noontime intramural basketball game or getting an A on an exam.

Don't you agree that it feels even better to "win" when the exam has been tough, when it's been challenging and difficult, than when it was one of Mr. Bibble's easy unit tests?

Vince got it right. Wanting to win is important. Otherwise, why would you study so hard and give up so much for so long?

Now that you've done the studying and taken the test, you want to know the results.

Let's assume you did well. Congratulations! But, no matter how many points you earned, reviewing the test is a vitally important exercise in preparing yourself for the next test—and for taking a hard look at the way you study.

If you take a standardized test and have the chance to get a copy of the exam—and your own answers—do so. It may cost you a few bucks, but I definitely think it's worth it. It's unlikely you'll find they made any mistakes in the scoring of the exam, but it will be good exercise for you to review what you got right and what you didn't while the test is reasonably fresh in your mind.

The emphasis in this chapter, however, is on the tests you take from teachers. Most will review the overall results of the test with the class on the day they are returned. First of all, you want to make sure the answers that you missed are truly incorrect. Teachers make mistakes. I know that comes as a shock.

Don't become a nuisance by challenging everything in class, waving your hand and saying, in a pleading voice, "But, but, Mr. Squeezicks! I meant to say George Washington Carver instead of George Washington!"

Concentrate on the answers that are clearly marked wrong. Even a semi-alert student evaluating his or her own exam can grab a couple of extra points, and those points might move you up another letter grade.

If the question really was ambiguous and your answer could arguably be as correct as the one the teacher chose, go ahead and make a pitch. This will be especially effective if a few others in the class chose the same answer. There *is* strength in numbers.

Let's suppose you got the answer wrong, fair and square. Most likely, you got it wrong for one of these reasons:

You made a careless mistake

1. You wrote down the wrong letter or number.
2. Similarly, you filled in the wrong box in the answer sheet.
3. You left out a whole section of the test because you didn't turn the page, or you "thought" you had done it, or...
4. You wrote in such a scribbled fashion or crammed the words together so much that the teacher pulled an "I can't read it so it's wrong" deal on you and gave you no credit.
5. You misread the directions. You missed the slightly important word "not," so you provided the exact opposite of what you should have.
6. You guessed wildly without even reading the options and ignored the fact that points would be deducted for wrong answers, so you got fewer points than if you had left the answer sheet blank for those questions.

You didn't know the material

1. You didn't read all the assignments, or get a complete set of notes, or find out answers to questions you had about some of the information.
2. You attended class, took notes, and read the assignments, but you didn't understand what the topic was all about.
3. You needed to know a lot of facts—dates, names, events, causes and effects—and you didn't.

Your personal life got in the way

1. You brought into the test your worries that the person you're dating is going to dump you, that your parents are fighting again, that your kids are heading to reform school if you don't do something right now.
2. You had a horrible cold, had a terrible headache, or you got too little or too much sleep.

Next time you'll know better

Don't beat up on yourself too much. Do take time to evaluate how you did—the bad and the good. Maybe you always hated essay questions and this time you did well. It's as important to evaluate why you *were* successful as why you *weren't*.

In that case, maybe you learned a lot from your study group. Maybe your teacher gave you some good advice. Maybe you read that section of this book first and it helped you (I like that choice). Maybe you're picking up reading and comprehension skills from a combination of factors. Think back over what you may have done differently this time. Give yourself a lot of the credit. After all, you took the test all by yourself. Pat-on-the-back time!

The worrisome part is the "careless mistake" area, yet it's probably the easiest to correct, too. Take a vow that you won't do such silly things again. It's especially annoying when you had the right answer and you simply circled the wrong one. Next time, pay a little closer attention to what you're doing and pace yourself so you can double-check your work.

There's no substitute for knowledge

If you go into the test knowing only half the material, don't expect to get above the 50-percent mark. Doing well on a test, as I've been telling you all along, is a combination of knowing how to take the test and knowing the stuff that goes into the answers.

If you can't seem to get prepared, maybe you'd better go back and reread those earlier chapters. Get to class, get your work organized, manage your time, read the book, do your homework, the whole *shtick*.

Now's the time to see where the teacher got the questions that made up the test. What percentage of the test came from the lectures? From the book? From handouts?

It is unlikely that you're going to get an A in every class you take, but you can get the best grade possible. Even in classes that, for whatever reason, are way, way over your head, you can at least pass. In most cases, you're going to do a lot better than that.

Ask questions. Ask questions during class. Ask questions when you meet with your teacher. Join a study group and ask questions. Ask questions when the test results are being discussed.

Guess how you did

Don't forget to see how many of your guesses you got right. Naturally, the better you know the material, the fewer guesses you need to make, but on some big tests you may make a lot of them.

Let's try that one again, shall we?

If you really messed up the test, sit down with your teacher and discuss the reasons (having done your self-evaluation, based on the areas mentioned in this chapter).

Ask if you can take another test—you may not be able to get any credit for it, but you'll impress him and he will look more kindly upon you when it comes time to enter your final grade on the official form.

Retaking "bad" tests is a good idea for another reason. Unless you just completely messed up in getting the right answers matched to the right questions, you probably performed so poorly because you didn't know the material well enough the first time.

Now you are giving yourself a second chance to learn material that will no doubt appear on future tests, and—now this may come as a real shock—you might actually need to know this information for some reason in your future life.

A satisfactory completion of the retake will give you that boost of self-confidence that got stomped on when you got a bad grade the first time. "Hey," you're saying to the Test Demons, "I can do this!"

But don't miss the test entirely (unless you're on your death bed, of course) or you'll face the wrath of Mrs. Khan—the make-up exam. Think a lot of teachers look forward to creating an entirely new test *just for you?* That they're going to make it *easier* than the test you missed? Or that they'll spend *less time* with your test at home than the weekend they had to grade 30? Think you want to stay as far away from Mrs. Khan's make-up tests as Ricardo Montalban?

Good answer.

Why do teachers choose essay questions?

1. They are quicker and easier to prepare.
2. They may be preferred when a group is small and the test will not be reused.
3. They are used to explore students' attitudes rather than measure their achievements.
4. They are used to encourage and reward the development of the students' skill in writing.
5. They are suitable when it's important for the students to explain or describe.
6. They are more suitable to some material. You're likely to have more essay questions in English and history than you are in the sciences.

Teachers use objective questions because:

1. They are preferred when the group is large and the test may be reused.
2. They are more efficient when highly reliable test scores must be obtained quickly.
3. They are more suitable for covering a larger amount of content in the same amount of time.
4. They are easier for the teacher to give an impartial grade. Every student has to write down "C" to get number 22 correct.
5. They are easier for some teachers to create.
6. They may be used when students need to demonstrate or show.

A thousand points of right

At the time the teacher decides what kinds of questions she will ask and determines what each question will cover, she must also assign a point value to each question.

She will assign higher point values to questions that are concerned with material that has been emphasized in lectures, class discussions, and readings. She'll also assign more points to areas that require more time and attention.

Think about it: You've never taken a test where each true-false question was worth 20 points and the long essay was worth five. She will clearly show the points possible for each section and/or question so you can decide how to spend your time. (And if she doesn't, ask!)

Teachers have checklists, too

The teacher has selected the material to be covered. She's told you, at least in general terms, what the test will cover. She has decided on the format, assigned points, and written the questions, then double-checked to make sure she has included everything she wanted to include.

She has made sure the questions are different from those on previous tests, as she suspects that some of you will look at them, hoping she'll use the same questions.

She has set up the test in a format so there is no confusion, made sure it is free of typos, and checked her questions and answers to make sure they're not ambiguous.

Should we give her a passing grade?

The "test" for her comes when she sits down to grade what you've done. If half the students completely messed up one of the questions—but messed it up in the same way—she has to admit that the directions were not clearly written. She may even decide to throw out the question.

She has determined that the number and complexity of the questions are suitable for the time allotted for the test. If she consistently finds that even her best students only completed half the test, she had too much material on the test, and, hopefully, will shorten future ones.

A key word that the teacher has to remind herself to use in making up and grading a test is "reasonable." What is a *reasonable* number of questions students can be expected to answer in 45 minutes? What should a teacher *reasonably* expect students to know from the chapters?

You can learn to fake sincerity

No, you can't. I just said that to keep your attention. Let me leave you with this thought about your relationship with your teachers: Teachers like students (and give them better grades) if they show genuine interest in the subject and the class. You don't have to be a teacher's pet or Nerd of the Month, but if you like what you're learning, show it.

If you've decided that chemistry is up on your dislike list along with public speaking and major leg cramps, don't vent your anger and snide remarks to your teacher. He loves this stuff. He even goes to conventions where there are other chemistry teachers. He spends his weekends reading books such as *50 Ways to Make Milkshakes with Hydrochloric Acid.* Just endure. Do the best you can, and, best of all, go to him with honest questions about material that you don't understand. He's there to help you.

Fill in the blank so you won't go blank

I'll leave you with one more thing—the item I referred to in Chapter 4. On pages 118 and 119 is the form I've designed to help you sort out what you've got to do when, where, and how. Photocopy it, then fill in the blanks.

There. I've said it. I'm done. You're just getting started.

Don't ever say again, "She gave me a C!" No, *she* didn't. You give yourself the grades you deserve, the grades you earn by either studying or goofing off. So what grade are you going to give yourself next time?

Pre-Test Organizer

Class:____________________**Teacher:**________________

Test date:_____________**Time:** From________to________

Place: ____

Special instructions to myself (take calculator, dictionary, etc.): ____________________________________

____

Materials I need to study for this test (check all needed):

- ❑ Book
- ❑ Workbook
- ❑ Class notes
- ❑ Handouts
- ❑ Tapes/videos
- ❑ Old tests
- ❑ Other____________________

Format of the test will be (write the number of T/F, essays, etc., and total points for each section):

____

____

____

____

____

____

____

Study group meetings (times, places):

1. ____

2. ____

3. ____

4. ____

5. ____

Index

"ACE" ANY TEST

A

B

C

D

E

F

G

I

K

L

M

N

O

P

R

S

T

U

NOTES

NOTES

NOTES